*Economic Development
and Growth*

Introduction to Economics Series

Kenyon A. Knopf, *Editor*

NATIONAL INCOME AND EMPLOYMENT ANALYSIS, 2ND ED.
Arnold Collery

THE MARKET SYSTEM, 2ND ED.
Robert H. Haveman and Kenyon A. Knopf

INTERNATIONAL ECONOMIC PROBLEMS, 2ND ED.
James C. Ingram

THE ECONOMICS OF POVERTY, 2ND ED.
Alan B. Batchelder

THE ECONOMICS OF THE PUBLIC SECTOR
Robert H. Haveman

ECONOMIC DEVELOPMENT AND GROWTH, 2ND ED.
(1972)
Robert E. Baldwin

CASE STUDIES IN AMERICAN INDUSTRY, 2ND ED.
Leonard W. Weiss

TOWARD ECONOMIC STABILITY
Maurice W. Lee

WELFARE AND PLANNING: AN ANALYSIS OF
CAPITALISM VERSUS SOCIALISM
Heinz Kohler

URBAN ECONOMICS
William L. Henderson and Larry C. Ledebur

Economic Development and Growth

ROBERT E. BALDWIN

University of Wisconsin

SECOND EDITION

John Wiley & Sons, Inc.
New York • London • Sydney • Toronto

Library of Congress Cataloging in Publication Data:

Baldwin, Robert E.
    Economic development and growth.

    (Introduction to economics series)
    Bibliography: p.
    1. Economic development. I. Title.

HD82.B26   1972   338.9   70-39119
ISBN 0-471-04591-8
ISBN 0-471-04592-6 (pbk.)

Printed in the United States of America

10 9 8 7 6 5 4 3 2 1

Introduction to Economics Series

Teachers of introductory economics seem to agree on the impracticality of presenting a comprehensive survey of economics to freshman or sophomores. Many of them believe there is a need for some alternative which provides a solid core of principles while permitting an instructor to introduce a select set of problems and applied ideas. This series attempts to fill that need and also to give the interested layman a set of self-contained books that he can absorb with interest and profit, without assistance.

By offering greater flexibility in the choice of topics for study, these books represent a more realistic and reasonable approach to teaching economics than most of the large, catchall textbooks. With separate volumes and different authors for each topic, the instructor is not as tied to a single track as in the omnibus introductory economics text.

Underlying the series is the pedagogical premise that students should be introduced to economics by learning how economists think about economic problems. Thus the concepts and relationships of elementary economics are presented to the student in conjunction with a few economic problems. An approach of this kind offers a good beginning to the student who intends to move on to advanced work and furnishes a clearer understanding for those whose study of economics is limited to an introductory exposure. Teachers and students alike should find the books helpful and stimulating.

Kenyon A. Knopf, Editor

Preface

The topic of economic development, like so many other economic subjects, is presented to students either in a very brief and superficial way in the standard elementary economics textbook or in a detailed theoretical manner, replete with graphs and equations, in intermediate texts devoted entirely to development. The student discovers what the problem is and learns a few cliches in the elementary course, but little else. The intermediate course covers the subject well enough, but it is usually open only to advanced economics majors because of its theoretical nature. Consequently, only a very small fraction of those who take at least one course in economics learn more than a few highly simplified notions about the development process.

The purpose of this book is to provide an analysis of economic development that in terms of breadth and sophistication lies between the usual elementary and advanced approaches to the development topic. Without the space restrictions of the elementary textbook, the main parts of the subject can be explored in some depth. However, this will be done without using any more elaborate analytical tools and concepts than are developed in the theoretical parts of the standard elementary course. As is the case with most subjects in economics, it turns out that the development topic can be covered quite adequately with the elementary kit of analytical tools. Too often, advanced theory is used simply to avoid taking the time to explain carefully a concept in common-sense terms.

This book is organized around three general questions: (1) What is the nature of the growth problem facing the less developed countries? (2) What are the main theories concerning the key relationships that determine a country's rate and pattern of development? (3) What are the major policies issues with which less developed countries must currently deal, and what is the best way of handling these issues?

The first question is covered in Chapter 1 where, by contrasting the developed and less developed countries, an economic profile of the latter countries is given. The next four chapters survey what we know about how economic development takes place. It covers not only some of the main contributions of recent years, but also the development theories of such earlier writers as Adam Smith, Marx, and Schumpeter. Finally, the next three chapters are devoted to applying the analytical knowledge to the pressing and difficult policy questions that the developing countries must try to answer. The last chapter then deals with some of the policy lessons that we have learned in recent years as well as the prospects for growth in the less developed countries.

ROBERT E. BALDWIN

Contents

1

Progress and Poverty

Since 1945 economic development has become a major social and political issue in world affairs. This is not due to any sudden discovery of the extent of poverty in the world, but rather to a change in social attitudes towards its existence. The facts on poverty have always been available—at least in general outline—for anyone who cared to look at them. The difficulty has been to get governments and private individuals to regard widespread poverty as a condition that requires urgent and significant efforts to alleviate. This view was not generally accepted until after the Second World War when most colonial territories had achieved their political independence. After becoming free of external control, these emerging nations immediately set out after higher living standards, and most instituted domestic reforms designed to stimulate economic growth. Rightly or wrongly, many citizens of these new countries believed that the developed countries had not only tended to neglect the economic welfare of most of the population in the less developed economies, but also that the advanced countries had used their greater economic and political power to obtain an "unfair" share of the income gains from doing business with the less developed nations.

The developed countries have responded to the economic aspirations of the developing nations[1] by making substantial

---

[1] The term "developing" countries will be used interchangeably with "less developed," "underdeveloped," and "poor" countries. The "developed" countries will also be referred to as "advanced" and "rich" countries.

contributions of capital funds, manpower, and technical knowledge to them. In 1968, for example, the net flow of long-term
capital (public and private) and official donations to the developing nations amounted to $13 billion. The United States alone
furnished 45%, or nearly $6 billion, of this amount.

Although most of the discussion of economic development
focuses upon raising per capita income levels, there is also an
appreciation of the importance of maintaining high-growth rates
for achieving other major economic and social goals. A vigorously expanding economy is not only the best insurance against
unemployment for a given labor force, but is essential for ab-
sorbing, without painful adjustments, the large number of new
entrants who enter the work force each year. The ability to
strengthen social welfare programs for such groups as the
elderly, the sick, and the poorly educated is also much easier,
if the needed funds can be obtained by taking a portion of the
increase in national income rather than by taking a larger share
of a fixed income stream. The importance to the developing
countries of rapid growth in the advanced countries—and vice
versa—should also be emphasized. The developed countries purchase over 90% of the exports of the developing countries, and
unless income levels in the former countries rise rapidly the
developing countries tend to suffer from conditions of oversup-
ply. High-growth rates in the developing countries are also an
important stimulant to the exports of capital goods from the
developed countries.

The economics of development is the study of the key economic relationships that determine the levels and growth rates
of per capita income in less developed nations. There are some
differences in the way various writers divide countries into developed and less developed (or developing) nations, but one
widely followed classification divides all countries into developed
market economies, centrally planned economies, and developing
market economies. The first group includes: Canada, the United
States, Western Europe, the Republic of South Africa, Japan,
Australia, and New Zealand. The centrally planned economies
are: the USSR, Eastern Europe, mainland China, North Korea,
North Viet-Nam, Mongolia and Cuba. The rest of the world
makes up the developing market economies. We shall be con-

cerned in this book with this last group of countries. There are a number of countries in the centrally planned group that are similar to developing market economies in terms of income levels and the nature of their productive structures, but we shall not analyze the methods used to stimulate growth in these nations. This is another extensive topic in itself.

The first step in studying the growth process in developing economies is to obtain a general economic picture of these nations. Such a survey not only brings out the nature of their development problems, but also suggests the kind of economic changes that are likely to be necessary if development in these countries is to be successful. A useful way of presenting this survey is to contrast the developing countries with the developed nations. In this chapter differences between the two groups will be illustrated not only with regard to living standards and growth rates but also with respect to the structure of production and the quantitative and qualitative nature of their basic means of production.

I. THE INCOME GAP

The tremendous gap in economic well-being between the rich and poor parts of the world is best brought out by per capita income estimates (Tables 1-1 and 1-2). For the less developed market economies as a whole, per capita output in 1969 averaged only $200 compared to over $2600 in the developed nations. This meant that over 83% of all goods and services were produced in countries where only 27% of the world's population lived.

A person brought up in a developed country finds it almost impossible to understand how anyone can survive on an income as low as $200 per year. In the United States, even if one "lived on bread alone," he would end up with not much more than a loaf a day. Actually, experts who calculate dollar estimates of income levels point out that the standard figures do understate living standards in less developed nations. Most income estimates undervalue the goods and services produced in the rural sector of developing economies where many commodities are never exchanged for money. In addition, there is considerable evidence that converting a developing country's gross national product

Table 1-1. Growth Rates of Per Capita Gross National Product and Growth Rates of Population by Regions

	Annual Average Growth Rates			
	Per Capita GNP (in constant prices)			Population
	1955–60	1960–65	1965–69	1965–69
Less developed countries				
Total	2.3%	2.6%	3.2%	2.6%
Latin America	2.2	2.0	2.5	2.9
Near East	3.4	4.1	4.3	2.4
South Asia	2.1	1.3	2.3	2.5
Far East	1.2	2.8	4.9	2.7
Africa	n.a.	1.1	2.4	2.5
Other	2.3	6.8	5.0	1.1
Developed countries				
Total including U. S.	2.2	4.0	3.9	0.9
Total excluding U. S.	3.9	4.5	4.8	0.9
United States	0.5	3.3	3.1	1.1
Europe	3.6	3.9	3.7	0.6
Other developed countries	4.3	6.3	7.6	1.4

Source. *Gross National Product: Growth Rates and Trend Data,* Office of Statistics and Reports, Agency for International Development.

expressed in its own currency into dollar terms by using the free-market dollar price of the currency gives insufficient weight to the value of the noninternationally traded goods produced in the country. One study concludes that because of such factors the income estimates of the poorest countries should be tripled to present a more accurate picture of relative incomes.

Yet, even after doubling or tripling these figures, it is still difficult to appreciate their real meaning. Knowing how an average family in a particular less developed country spends its money may be helpful. In Rhodesia a budget survey of African employees working in Salisbury showed that the median earnings per family of five was $518. Food accounted for 50% of this sum. Furthermore, four foodstuffs—meat, bread, mealie meal (corn meal) and sugar—made up over two-thirds of these expenditures. Rent was the next largest expenditure item, amount-

Table 1-2. Levels and Growth Rates of Per Capita Gross National Product and Growth Rates of Population, Selected Countries

Country	Level of Per Capita GNP, 1969 (1968 prices)	Annual Average Growth Rates, 1965–69	
		Per Capita GNP (in constant prices)	Population
North America			
Canada	$3286	3.2%	1.7%
Mexico	572	3.1	3.5
United States	4380	2.8	1.7
South America			
Brazil	354	5.8	3.0
Chile	616	1.4	1.9
Peru	371	1.4	3.1
Venezuela	949	1.5	3.5
Asia			
India	87	2.2	2.5
Japan	1571	12.2	1.0
Philippines	208	2.8	3.5
Taiwan	322	7.4	2.5
Iran	314	6.5	3.1
Europe			
France	2724	5.4	0.8
Italy	1484	4.8	0.8
Africa			
Ethiopia	64	1.4	2.3
Ghana	244	0.2	2.8
Morocco	197	2.4	3.2
Uganda	100	5.2	2.5
Oceania			
Australia	2380	4.7	1.8

Source. Gross National Product: Growth Rates and Trend Data, Office of Statistics and Reports, Agency for International Development.

ing to 22% of the family budget. Clothing and footwear (10%); such household items as soap, blankets, and furniture (6%); and fuel and light (5%—mainly firewood and paraffin) made up another 21%. The remaining portion of this typical family's budget went for drink and tobacco, a bicycle, and miscellaneous items. Only 2% of the family's income of $518 was saved.

The wide gap between living standards in developed versus developing countries is also brought out by nonmonetary indications of economic well-being (Table 1-3). For example, whereas the average person born today in a developed country will live to 70 years of age, life expectancy in most developing countries is only about 50 years. After one looks at the differences in nutrition or in the number of people a doctor must care for, the fact that such divergences in average length of life exist is no surprise.

A. Is the Gap Widening?

Is the income gap between rich and poor nations widening? Marxists have long predicted that such a widening is an inevitable outcome of capitalist exploitation. They say it will continue until the underdeveloped nations join with the working classes of the advanced nations to destroy the capitalistic system. Quite aside from the scientific content of Marx's prediction, there is little doubt that in these days of mass communication any increase in the gap between rich and poor nations tends to generate feelings of resentment and injustice. These attitudes may lead to political instability and change in the underdeveloped countries—factors which can prove highly costly to the long-run foreign policy interests of the developed countries.

And the fact is that the gap does appear to be widening. As Table 1-1 indicates, except for the 1955–1960 period, per capita income has grown faster in the developed countries over the last 15 years than in the developing economies. Since 1960, for example, per capita income has increased about 10% more in the developed than in the less developed countries. In view of the rather wide margins of error involved in measuring total output changes and population growth, the figures should be regarded as only approximate. Nevertheless, the difference seems sufficiently large to warrant the conclusion that the gap is widening. Indeed, what data are available suggest that the per capita income gap between the developed and developing groups has been widening over at least the last 70 years.

Although per capita output is growing faster in the developed than in the underdeveloped countries, the opposite is true regarding gross national product. In the period 1965–1969, for

Table 1-3. Nonmonetary Indicators of Living Standards

	Life Expectancy (years)	People Per Physician	Calories Per Day	Literacy Rate (percent)	Students as Percent of 5–19 Age Group	Electric Power Per Capita (KWH per yr.)	Persons Per Square Mile
Developed areas	70	750	2920	96	77	4520	52
United States	70	670	3090	98	87	7120	56
Less developed areas	51	3800	2230	40	38	180	70
Africa	40	17,600	2310	20	25	80	25
East Asia	49	4500	2120	58	44	110	190
Latin America	59	1700	2560	68	46	440	33
Near East and South Asia	50	4800	2120	29	35	100	175

Source. *Economic Growth Trends*, Office of Statistics and Reports, Agency for International Development.

example, gross national product (in real terms) grew at an average rate of 5.8% annually as compared to 4.9% in the developed countries. The gap in per capita income widened because population increased at only 0.9% annually in the developed countries compared to a 2.6% annual rate in the less developed economies.

The view that it is the collective responsibility of people in developed countries to help narrow the gap in living standards rests on the growing acceptance of the notion that we live in a world community as well as a national community, and should, therefore, be concerned about the welfare of all mankind. The moral obligation for those who have to share with those who have not cannot sensibly be limited to one's national borders. Moreover, in today's highly interdependent world, we simply cannot ignore the economic and social problems of other countries. Pollution of the environment in one country can significantly affect the quality of life in other countries. Epidemics and diseases now quickly spread from one country to another. Such foreign economic conditions as droughts, depressions, and resource depletions also are becoming increasingly important to all nations because of their impact on the quantities and prices of internationally traded goods.

Although the widening income gap should be taken as a signal of the need for greater efforts in both developed and developing countries to accelerate the pace of growth in the latter countries, it should also be recognized that there has been substantial absolute progress in these countries during the last two decades. Raising living standards even moderately in the underdeveloped world has not proved to be the almost unachievable objective it seemed to many in the late forties. For example, as is discussed in more detail in the next section, the age-old stagnation in agriculture in the developing countries seems on the verge of being broken. Transportation and communication facilities have been spectacularly improved. Although still a comparatively small part of developing countries' total production, manufacturing output has grown at a 7.3% rate in these countries during the sixties as compared to 5.6% in the industrialized nations. The gap in primary and secondary school enrollment between the two groups has also been narrowing. Similarly, in the last two decades gains in life expectancy have been achieved in less developed areas that took a century to accomplish in the developed nations.

B. The Population Explosion
Versus the Green Revolution

To many observers, man's short-run economic future is vastly more bleak than just a growing income gap between rich and poor nations. To use Paul Ehrlich's words, "In the 1970's the world will undergo famines—hundreds of millions of people are going to starve to death in spite of any crash programs embarked upon now."[2] Although in the view of such writers as Ehrlich, the population problem is worldwide, its most pressing present aspect is the pressure exerted in the developing countries on available food supplies.

When one considers that the population of the less developed countries as a whole (2.4 billion) will double by the year 2000 even if fertility rates are considerably reduced, it is difficult not to become alarmed. How is it going to be possible to feed all of these additional people adequately? We know, for example, that as recently as 1965 and 1966 India suffered food famines when per capita production fell over 15% due to severe droughts. On the other hand, there has been much talk recently about "miracle" rice and the "Green Revolution." Those writing about these topics often seem more concerned with the problem of overproduction of food cereals in the seventies than overpopulation of people. Which of these seemingly contradictory positions is correct?

The facts on the population explosion are strikingly clear. Prior to the 1950's, population growth in the less developed countries was characterized by high birth rates and high death rates with the result that growth rates usually were between 1 and 1.5% annually. However, the discovery of antibiotics and improvements in public health measures dramatically reduced death rates. In Puerto Rico, for example, the death rate was nearly cut in half in just 10 years. Birth rates, on the other hand, have continued to remain at their high levels so that growth rates in population of 2.5–3.0% annually are now typical (see Table 1-4).

---

[2] Paul R. Ehrlich, *The Population Bomb*, New York: Ballantine Books, 1968, Prologue.

European experience in the last century suggests that a decline in birth rates follows a drop in death rates after a lag period, but so far there is evidence of such a fall in birth rates only in a few countries.

Despite the rapid growth in population, the trends of both total per capita outputs and per capita food production have managed to remain upward in the postwar period. Fluctuations around the trend of per capita food production have been extensive, however. For example, the drought on the subcontinent

Table 1-4. Birth and Death Rates[a]

Country	Crude Birth Rate (Per 1000)	Crude Death Rate (Per 1000)	Natural Rate of Increase (Per 1000)
North America			
Canada	17.7	7.7	10.3
Mexico	43.5	9.6	33.9
United States	17.4	9.6	7.8
South America			
Argentina	22.3	8.7	13.6
Brazil	41–43	10–12	29–33
Chile	30.9	9.5	21.4
Peru	44–45	12–14	30–33
Asia			
Burma	50	35	15
India	41.7	22.8	18.9
Japan	18.5	6.8	11.7
Taiwan	29.3	5.5	23.8
Europe			
France	16.8	11.0	5.8
Italy	17.6	10.1	7.5
Africa			
Ghana	47–52	24	23–28
Morocco	46.1	18.7	27.4
Rhodesia	48.1	14.0	34.1
Oceania			
Australia	20.0	9.1	10.9

[a] The data refer mainly to either the year 1967 or 1968. For several developing countries, however, the data cover some period in the 1960's.
Source. United Nations, *Demographic Yearbook, 1968,* New York, 1969, pp. 103–111 and United Nations, *Statistical Yearbook, 1969,* New York, 1970, pp. 72–77.

of India in the mid-sixties reduced per capita food production for the developing countries as a whole to the mid-fifties level. Partly as a response to this crisis but, more importantly, as a result of the introduction of high-yield new varieties of wheat and rice that were developed by scientists with the Rockefeller and Ford Foundations, food production has risen dramatically since that period. In India and Pakistan, wheat production rose 74 and 85%, respectively, between 1966 and 1969, whereas rice production increased in Ceylon and West Pakistan 41 and 53%, respectively, between 1966 and 1968. It is estimated that India will be able to feed her large and expanding population by 1972.

Does the Green Revolution mean that we no longer need be concerned about the population problem? With respect to outright famines it does appear to be true that the outlook, for the 1970's at least, is much brighter than predicted by Ehrlich. However, in the long run, most experts seem to regard the Green Revolution as only buying additional time, perhaps 15 to 30 years, in which to develop the will and techniques for effective worldwide population control. Furthermore, there will still be a population problem in this interval, but it will take the form of the need to provide sufficient jobs for the young people who represent the initial waves of the population explosion rather than providing sufficient food for these people.

There are, on the other hand, some highly qualified agricultural and population experts who think this view is either much too optimistic or much too pessimistic. Our degree of success in predicting in this field is sufficiently poor that it would be unwise to dismiss casually either viewpoint. The pessimists contend that much of the recent increase in food output has been due to exceptionally favorable weather conditions and costly government subsidy programs. They are also skeptical about the possibilities of successfully introducing the new high-yielding varieties of food in more than a comparatively few areas because of the problem of providing adequate irrigation water and they warn of the dangers of devastating plant diseases. The optimists, on the other hand, see no serious population problems either in the short or in the long run. Basically, they believe that man has the ability to produce the technology needed to avert all food problems related to a rapidly growing world population. Inevitably this view involves the belief that man will be able not only to vastly increase the output of all types of goods and services but also to undertake space settlement successfully on satellites and other planets. The vision of the optimists is that man is destined to populate a universe of unlimited size. However, even if one grants that the food problem can be solved for a long time into the future or perhaps permanently, there still remains an entire set of important issues concerning the quality of life not only in relation to pollution problems but more generally in relation to the irritations of living in a crowded environment.

II. STRUCTURAL DIFFERENCES IN PRODUCTION PATTERNS

A. *The Agricultural Sector*

Data showing differences in levels and growth rates of output and population only begin to tell the story of the economic distinctions between the rich and poor countries. Besides changes in levels and growth rates of aggregate output, there are significant differences in the composition of total output. Without doubt, the most striking difference is the much higher proportion of total output generated in agriculture in less developed coun-

Table 1-5. Origin of Gross Domestic Product and Distribution of Economically Active Population, by Industry Groups

Country		Agriculture, Forestry, and Fishing (%)	Mining, Manufacturing, Construction, and Electricity (%)	All Other (%)
North America				
Canada	A[a]	6	38	56
	B[b]	11	34	55
Mexico	A	16	37	47
	B	54	19	27
United States	A	3	37	60
	B	6	34	60

[a] A, origin of GDP. The data refer in most cases to either 1962 or 1963.
[b] B, distribution of population. The years covered vary between 1960 and 1964.

Table 1-5. (*Continued*)

Country		Agriculture, Forestry, and Fishing (%)	Mining, Manufacturing, Construction, and Electricity (%)	All Other (%)
South America				
Brazil	A	30	27	43
	B	52	25	23
Chile	A	8	43	49
	B	28	28	44
Peru	A	20	28	52
	B	50	19	31
Asia				
India	A	52	19	29
	B	73	11	16
Japan	A	12	36	52
	B	24	32	44
Philippines	A	33	24	43
	B	53	14	33
South Korea	A	35	24	41
	B	50	18	32
Europe				
France	A	9	48	43
	B	20	37	43
Italy	A	12	40	48
	B	22	46	32
Africa				
Sudan	A	54	12	34
	B	86	8	6
United Arab	A	28	27	45
Republic	B	57	12	11
Zambia	A	9	53	38
	B	5	38	57
Oeania				
Australia	A	11	41	48
	B	9	39	52

Source. Origin of GDP: United Nations, *Yearbook of National Accounts Statistics, 1968,* Vol. II, New York, 1969, pp. 83–100. Occupational Distribution: International Labour Office, *Yearbook of Labour Statistics, 1969,* Geneva, 1970, pp. 42–139.

tries (Table 1-5). In most developed countries less than 10% of the economy's output originates in agriculture, whereas 30–50% is the typical range in developing nations.

The share of the labor force engaged in agricultural pursuits also brings out this structural difference between developed and less developed economies even more strikingly (Table 1-5). In the United States, for example, only 6.5% of the economically active population is engaged in agricultural activities in contrast to 72.9% in India. The data for developed and underdeveloped countries is not completely comparable, however. A peasant producer in an underdeveloped country not only grows his products but also is likely to transport them to market and even to sell them himself. He and his family also build their own home and make many of the household utensils they use. Yet, instead of the individual being listed as engaged partly in transportation, trading, construction, and manufacturing activities, he is classified as being entirely in agriculture under the usual occupational statistics. His counterpart in developed countries, on the other hand, has become highly specialized. He hires others to transport his commodities and to build his house and furniture. Thus, these nonagricultural activities are separately identified in the statistics of the developed countries.

Another aspect of the low degree of specialization in the rural sector of less developed countries is the relatively small volume of trade within this sector as well as with other parts of the economy. A large part of the rural sector is a subsistence economy. Each household produces a small surplus for sale in order to obtain such items as clothing and agricultural tools, but the bulk of what is produced is consumed by the family or sold within the village.

The productive techniques used in the rural, subsistence sector are extremely crude. In parts of Central Africa, for example, subsistence farmers still follow a slash and burn cultivation method known as the *chitemene* system. Branches of nearby trees are cut off and piled to a height of about two feet over an area of nearly two acres. Just before the rainy season begins, the entire pile is set afire and such seeds as millet, pumpkin, and squash are scattered in the ashes. The only other work required before harvesting is the building of a fence to protect the crops from wild animals. The garden is not abandoned for three or four years. This agricultural method has proven to be surprisingly productive but, since something like ten acres of woodlands is required for one acre of garden, it has become increasingly uneconomic as the population has increased. It is also incapable of supporting cash agricultural activities on any significant scale.

Underemployment of available labor resources is another widespread characteristic of the agriculture sector in the less developed world. A survey in South Korea reveals that the typical farm family is fully employed only in June, July, and October, and that approximately 30% of the total labor available annually is not used. Studies of Greece, southern Italy, and India give the same general results. Of course, seasonality of employment is a characteristic of agricultural activity in developed countries too. But periods during the year when farmers are idle or engaged in very low-productivity work are much less extensive. Economic development brings an increase in the range of alternative activities, and farmers in developed countries are better able to cope with the seasonal problem.

B. Production for Export

The other major distinction in the composition of production between developed and developing countries relates to their export trade. Less developed countries generally are "open" economies in the sense that exports constitute a significant fraction of the total value of domestic production. The same is true for many developed countries. What differs is that in developed countries exports are composed of many different important items, whereas one or two primary commodities usually dominate the export list of the developing nations. There are 30 developing countries (out of about 100) whose major single export in 1958 contributed at least 50% of their foreign exchange. They include Burma (rice, 60%); Ceylon (tea, 62%); Ghana (cocoa, 57%); Venezuela (oil, 93%); and Bolivia (tin, 62%). As a consequence both of the importance of exports in total production and of the high degree of export concentration, a significant fraction of national output in less developed countries is composed of one or two export items. While a lack of specialization is characteristic of the subsistence sector, a high degree of specialization is typical of the commercial sector. Less developed countries are, consequently, often aptly described as dualistic economies. In one part of the economy technologically advanced methods are employed to produce goods for cash markets. On the other hand, in the other—frequently much larger— part of the economy productive techniques are extremely crude and production is nonmarket oriented. The high degree of foreign ownership in the export sectors of many developing nations also contributes to the dualistic nature of these countries.

A heavy dependence on a few primary-product exports makes developing nations especially vulnerable to international market pressures. Wide supply shifts in agricultural commodities caused by climatic variations coupled with wide swings in demand due to business-cycle fluctuations in the advanced countries bring large short-run fluctuations in the export earnings of many developing countries. The discovery and exploration of alternative supply sources and the development of substitute products by the advanced countries can also significantly slow down an underdeveloped country's long-run growth. The impact of synthetic nitrates on Chile, of synthetic rubber on Malaya, and even of East African coffee production on Brazil illustrates this point. Resources in less developed countries are generally much less flexible than in developed countries. These countries consequently find it difficult to adapt to long-run changes in world supply and demand conditions.

One outcome that may have been due to this resource inflexibility is the apparent long-run decline in the ratio of the prices of the products underdeveloped countries sell to other nations (their exports) compared to the prices of commodities they buy from other countries (their imports), that is, the terms of trade of the less developed countries. Unfortunately, data on these relative prices over the last one hundred years is not sufficiently comprehensive to permit a definite statement about the trend of this price series. One point seems clear, however. The prices of primary commodities have not fallen over the long-run compared to prices of manufactured products. On the other hand, a series based on European trade indicates that the terms of trade of the less developed countries declined about 33% between

1900 and 1952. The two conclusions are consistent because, although underdeveloped countries are almost exclusively primary-product exporters, many developed countries also export substantial amounts of primary commodities such as coal and wheat. The evidence based on European countries cannot be considered conclusive, however. It does not cover all the trade of the less developed countries, and does not take account of the greater qualitative improvement in the manufactured commodities imported into the developing nations compared to the primary products exported by them. Furthermore, more comprehensive data collected by the United Nations indicate that between 1952 and 1969 there has been no significant trend in the terms of trade of the developing nations.

III. QUANTITATIVE AND QUALITATIVE DIFFERENCES IN THE MEANS OF PRODUCTION

Variations in the level and composition of per capita output among countries are manifestations of poverty and plenty. To understand the fundamental cause of these variations, however, it is necessary to examine the quantitative and qualitative characteristics of the basic productive factors in developed and developing countries.

A. *Labor*

One of the most striking demographic aspects of the population explosion is the increasing youthfulness of the population in developing countries. The recent decline in death rates, especially infant mortality rates, coupled with continued high birth rates, has increased the ratio of children to adults. Generally about 40% of the population is less than 15 years old in developing countries, whereas 30% or less is typical of developed countries. However, the relationship is reversed for people over 65 years of age—5% or less for developing countries and 8–10% for advanced nations. For the intermediate age group, that is, 15–64, the proportion is 63% in developed countries and 55% in developing nations. The implication for the developing countries of this smaller percentage of the most economically active population is that income per person for the whole population would be

lower in these countries than in the advanced economies even
if average productivity of those between 15 and 64 years of age
were the same. This can be offset by differences between the
groups of countries in the average ages at which individuals
begin to work and at which they retire, or in the proportion of
women who work, but there is no doubt that the higher depen-
dency ratio in developing countries is an important barrier to
raising per capita income levels.

Labor productivity, of course, is not the same in both groups
of countries but instead is much lower in the developing economies. Much of this is due to differences in the average quantity
of physical capital and land with which each laborer works in
developed versus less developed countries as well as to variations
in the nature of technology employed. However, there are also
differences in the efficiency of labor itself. Typical, for example,
are the results of a study of a machine tool plant in India indicating that three Indian workers were needed to match the output of two workers in a comparable plant in Switzerland. There
seem to be three main factors accounting for such variations in
the quality of the labor force: differences in the physical condition of the workers, differences in attitudes towards work, and
differences in levels of skill and education. The first factor is an
obvious consequence of poverty itself. Poverty, as well as those
institutional rigidities in developing countries that make it difficult for an individual to improve his social and economic position, also fosters work attitudes that are detrimental to efficiency.

Differences in skills and education levels, however, are the
most important factors accounting for the difference in relative
labor efficiency between developing and developed countries.
As Table 1-3 shows, only 40% of the population of developing
countries is literate in contrast to 96% in developed countries.
Furthermore, in most African and Latin American countries, for
example, more than one-half of primary school pupils do not
return to school after the second grade. However, in order to
take advantage in any significant manner of the income-raising
opportunities afforded by today's industrial technology, a country must possess comparatively plentiful supplies of trained,
educated workers. In many jobs in which modern technology is
employed it is not possible even to substitute a greater number

of unskilled workers to do the tasks of a skilled worker or technician. A certain minimum of skilled workers are needed, in other words, just to make production of many types of industrial products physically feasible—to say nothing of economically efficient. The considerable time and high costs involved in educating and training these more skilled workers and technicians make this requirement for industrial development *the* constraint that most limits the pace of economic growth in many developing countries.

B. Technology and Entrepreneurship

An extensive educational system is especially important in providing the researchers and specialized technicians who create new technology. The disparity in the amount of pure and applied research between advanced and underdeveloped nations is probably greater than for any other key requirement for growth. In the United States 4.2% of the gross national product is devoted to research and development (R & D) and in Europe the percentage is between 1 and 2%. On the other hand, in Latin America and Asia the figure is only 0.2 and 0.1–0.5%, respectively. In Africa, R & D expenditures are negligible. The adverse effects of this discrepancy in research expenditures, however, are mitigated somewhat by the flow of technological knowledge across national borders. But, outside of those export industries in which foreign investment is significant, there is a definite lag in the movement of this knowledge to the less developed countries. They seldom get in on the ground floor of new, highly profitable technological innovations. Furthermore, in many instances these countries do not have the trained personnel capable of exploiting the new technical opportunities.

Technological progress may be a necessary condition for economic progress but more than this is needed. There must be individuals who are willing to assume the risks of introducing new methods of production. Some economists believe that the absence of these entrepreneurs is the major explanation for the lack of rapid growth in some less developed countries. How large numbers of these individuals arise in an economy is only imperfectly understood, but it is clear that, where they exist, they play an important role in the development process. In Pakistan, for example, where industrial development has been very rapid in recent years, a small group of traders from a few villages suddenly and unexpectedly emerged to lead this industrial growth. In the Philippines the entrepreneurial group responsible for the establishment of large manufacturing units is generally comprised of the college-educated individuals from the upper stratum of large landowners, highly successful professionals, big businessmen, and top government officials. Some factors that seem to be important in creating an entrepreneurial group are discussed in Chapter 5. The point to make here is merely that there are significant differences among the developing countries in the extent to which this group exists. In the developed countries the function of entrepreneurship has become increasingly institutionalized in the large business unit. Many individuals participate in entrepreneurial activity, but only by specializing in a small part of the total process. Entrepreneurship in the less developed countries, on the other hand, is still more identifiable with particular individuals.

C. Natural Resources

Probably the oldest explanation for per capita income differences among nations is one that emphasizes variations in national resources. We sometimes hear that the fortunate combination of iron ore, coal, and limestone is the main reason the United Kingdom, Germany, and the United States were able to rise to industrial prominence. Or we are occasionally told that the climate of temperate zones is more conducive to energy and creativity than the weather in the tropics.

The trouble with such theories is that there are so many exceptions to their generalizations. A simple correlation between per capita income and such natural-resource factors as arable land per person or per capita supplies of various minerals does not yield a significant result. This is not because natural resources are unimportant for development, but because other productive factors such as capital, labor skills, and technology have enabled many nations to free themselves to a considerable extent from this ancient development constraint. But even in these countries, a lack of certain natural resources makes development efforts more difficult. In underdeveloped countries where the ratio of population to arable land already is comparatively high and where the population is increasing rapidly, the natural-resource constraint is particularly important. In Korea, for example, there are 12.8 persons per hectare of arable land compared to only 1 in Tanzania. In much of Tanzania it is still possible for a young man who wishes to set up his own farm simply to clear unused bushland. In Korea, on the other hand, a person in similar circumstances is likely to be able to earn a living only by becoming an agricultural laborer. Given the lack of capital in both countries and the difficulties of introducing more productive agricultural techniques, the extra degree of freedom in nations such as Tanzania makes their development problem considerably less severe both economically and socially than in countries like Korea.

Many people who are greatly concerned about the problem of feeding an exploding population also fear that we face disaster because of the exhaustion of natural resources. In some ways this appears to be even more serious than the food problem, since we can at least maintain food production with a constant population. However, even if population is held constant, we shall still gradually use up our supplies—at least on earth—of such natural resources as oil and coal. However, most economic geographers do not share the degree of concern about the natural-resource problem that this line of reasoning tends to generate. They stress the point that the notion of the supply of natural resources is only relevant in terms of a given technology. Technological improvements have created new resources and new products that substitute for old ones. For example, atomic power is increasingly being used to generate electricity rather than coal or water power. Plastics and synthetic fibers, which are made from raw materials that appear to be limitless in supply, are two other important illustrations of new products that have sharply altered the effective supply of natural resources meeting particular economic needs. Resource experts now maintain that there is no obvious reason why technological progress cannot in effect keep the supply of natural resources into the indefinite future adequate for rapid economic development.

This conclusion does not mean, however, that we do not face some serious problems in the natural-resource area. As increases in population and improvements in communications have increased the degree to which our individual economic and social actions are interrelated, we have rightly become more concerned about the unfavorable and uncompensated environmental effects of certain types of economic activity. For example, a firm that pollutes the atmosphere around its plants with smoke and fumes causes physical discomfort and perhaps serious injury to those living nearby. Yet, under a completely free price system there is likely to be no incentive for the firm to modify its actions or compensate those who are hurt. Special price incentives introduced by the government, e.g., taxes, subsidies, or stringent regulations, are needed to correct these situations.

As technological progress increases the supply of natural resources, care must be taken to guard against such undesirable environmental effects. In providing a cooling system for a nuclear power plant, for example, we must be sure that the one chosen by the power company as the cheapest from its viewpoint is not in fact among the most expensive ones when its total repercussions on others are taken into account. Such could be the case if the firm freely used the waters of some lake or river for cooling purposes.

D. Capital

Attempting to formulate any meaningful intercountry comparisons in the per capita stock of real capital is even more difficult than measuring natural-resource differences. Comparable estimates exist only for some advanced countries. For example, in 1964 the value of the net stock of structures and equipment per employee in France and Italy was only 54 and 36%, respectively, of that in the United States. The usual way of getting around this lack of comprehensive estimates is to enumerate differences among nations with respect to particular capital items, for example, per capita electrical power capacity (see Table 1-3) and number of tractors per rural resident. All have obvious drawbacks as representative indicators of a country's capital stock. The number of tractors per rural person, for example, exaggerates the difference between developed and developing countries in the capital stock available in the agricultural sector, since animals often take the place of tractors in developing countries. Even with generous allowances for such factors, the data indicate a tremendous gap in real capital supplies of developed versus less developed countries.

The usual practice of treating outlays for such services as education or health entirely as consumption expenditures means that even this gap is underestimated. We can quite properly argue that these expenditures raise a person's productivity as well as provide him with current utility. A complete measure of capital should include the investment in human beings that has been made in the past. Since expenditures of this kind have been larger in developed than in less developed regions, the gap in capital stock would be even wider than under traditional measuring procedures.

The crucial question concerning capital is how rapidly it is being accumulated in the developing countries. During the sixties, gross investment averaged about 18% of gross national product in these countries. In contrast, the gross investment ratio for the developed countries was about 21%. The ratio for the developing countries compares favorably with the 10% level that prevailed in the United States and Europe in the last century. However, though the accumulation of physical capital is a key factor in development, the lack of a strong positive correlation between investment ratios and growth rates in the sixties indicate it is not as important a factor as it was thought to be in the early fifties.

2

Traditional Development Theory and the Marxist Challenge

Facts describing the main differences in the structure and the means of production between developed and developing countries add to our knowledge of the conditions and sources of worldwide poverty, but they do little to increase understanding of how this poverty came about or how it can best be eliminated. To answer these questions, it is necessary to study the manner in which economic development takes place.

Economic development can best be conceived of as a dynamic, sequential process. Changes in one set of variables cause changes in other sets of variables, which in turn may bring about increases in per capita income. Nor need the process end there. An increase in income can itself set off repercussions that eventually result in a still further income rise. The problem both for those who wish to predict future per capita income accurately and for those who want to devise policies for accelerating development is to discover the *key* variables and relationships in the development process.

This chapter and the following three are devoted to this goal. In these chapters the great development theories of the last 200 years, as well as the major contributions since World War II will be outlined and evaluated. These theories contain the basic principles that have proved to be the most significant in terms of historical experience and political influence. Although they usually cannot be applied directly to the present underdeveloped world, each theory does stress some particular relationship which is essential for understanding the main processes of growth in today's developing nations.

The common denominator of the theories to be described in Chapters 2 and 3, which cover the period from the classical writers to the post-Keynesians, is their focus upon capital accumulation as the crucial process in economic development. All of these theories seek to understand both the process by which capital goods are amassed and the economic factors that foster or impede capital accumulation. The present chapter considers the contributions of the classical and neoclassical economists as well as of Marx with regard to these goals. As will be noted, the analysis of classical economists stands out because it shows how economic development can be thwarted by population pressures coupled with a scarcity of natural resources. The contribution of neoclassical writers, on the other hand, is significant for its improvement over classical economics in analyzing the saving and investment process and in tracing the intersector repercussions of development. Neoclassical writers, unlike Marx, also stress the favorable effects of technological progress. Marx contends that the relations of production associated with capitalism are incompatible with the technological progress generated under the system and, consequently, that capitalism will be plagued with periodic depressions and ultimate economic stagnation. Quite aside from the validity of these contentions, Marxian analysis is useful in pointing to the frequently high costs of development in terms of social and economic disruptions.

I. THE CLASSICAL VIEW

Without doubt, the best-known name in economics is Adam Smith. His monumental work, *An Inquiry into the Nature and Causes of the Wealth of Nations* (1776),[1] has had tremendous influence on scholars and policymakers alike. As the title of the book indicates, Smith was mainly concerned with the problem

---

[1] Adam Smith, *An Inquiry into the Nature and Causes of the Wealth of Nations,* E. Cannan (Ed.), New York: The Modern Library, 1937.

of economic development. He wanted to discover how economic growth came about and what factors and policies impede it.

A. *Division of Labor and Cumulative Growth*

According to Smith, division of labor was the key to increased productivity. When workers specialize in specific activities rather than undertake several production tasks, they can collectively produce more with the same effort. However, since the division of labor cannot take place on a large scale unless workers can use specialized machinery and equipment, Smith emphasizes the need for an economy to accumulate stocks of these capital goods in order to enjoy the benefits of higher per capita income levels. The ability to accumulate capital in turn depends upon the willingness of the people in the economy to devote a portion of the productive resources over which they have control to the production of capital goods rather than consumption goods, that is, their willingness to save and invest rather than consume their entire incomes.

Another limitation on division of labor is the size of the market. If markets are too small, demand will be insufficient to buy the goods produced under mass-production methods. Rising income levels tend to expand markets for most commodities; also, new customers can be found in other countries. As Smith said of the discovery of America: "By opening a new and inexhaustible market to all the commodities of Europe, it gave occasion to new divisions of labor and improvements of art, which, in the narrow circle of ancient commerce, could never have taken place for want of a market to take off the greater part of their produce."[2]

Once development begins, it tends to be self-sustaining. Given some initial capital stock and adequate market possibilities, division of labor and specialization occur and national income increases. This rise in income not only expands market opportunities, but also causes greater saving and investment. This sets the stage for still further division of labor and income growth. Another benefit from division of labor is an increased flow of new and better ideas for producing commodities. The capital

---

[2] Ibid., p. 416.

stock made possible by previous division of labor and specialization takes the form of better machines and equipment.

Is there any limit to this cumulative process of development? Unfortunately, there is, according to Smith. This occurs when an economy attains "that full complement of riches which the nature of its soil and climate, and its situation with respect to other countries, allowed it to acquire."[3] Smith was not very precise in explaining just how a stationary position is reached, but the factor that finally stops growth is a scarcity of natural resources. As an economy matures through capital accumulation and population growth, it becomes progressively more difficult to overcome the natural-resources barrier. Profit rates on capital fall until neither the incentive nor the means of further capital accumulation are present.

B. The Ricardian Model

It remained for David Ricardo, perhaps the most brilliant of the classical economists, to spell out the manner in which stagnation eventually presses down upon all economies.[4] Ricardo's vision of development is one in which the increasing difficulty of providing food for an expanding population finally grinds the growth process to a halt. It is a simple yet comprehensive theory with an all too apparent relevance to the overpopulated developing countries.

There are three major economic groups in the Ricardian model: capitalists, laborers, and landlords. Capitalists are those who direct and—by saving out of their profits—initiate the development process. As long as the profit rate is above some minimum, near-zero level, they continue to save and accumulate capital. The largest group, the laborers, do not own any implements of production but use those provided by the capitalists. The size of the labor force changes, depending upon the level of wages. There is, according to Ricardo, some "natural" real

---

[3] Ibid., p. 94.
[4] Ricardo's major work is *The Principles of Political Economy and Taxation* (1817). This has been published as the first volume of P. Sraffa (Ed.), *The Works and Correspondence of David Ricardo,* Cambridge: Cambridge University Press, 1951.

wage level, fixed by custom and habit, at which the laboring population will neither increase nor decrease. If wages rise above this level, the fall in the death rate brought about by better nutrition and health standards acts to increase the population. On the other hand, when real wages fall below their "natural" level, deaths exceed births and the population declines.

The last group is the landlord class, those who own the fixed supply of land and are able to charge rent for its use. Rent on any unit of land using a certain amount of labor and capital is equal to the differences between the output produced on this land and the output that could be produced with the same labor and capital on the poorest grade of land in use. This latter land will in effect be free land that any capitalist can use without paying rent. Consequently, landlords who own land that yields more than this marginal land will be able to collect as rent the difference in output between marginal and intramarginal lands in the competitive bidding among capitalists for better lands.

C. The Stationary State

Like Adam Smith, Ricardo regarded the growth process as self-generating—up to a point. To start the process, the profit rate must be positive. This induces capitalists to save a portion of their income. Both landlords and workers consume their entire income, according to Ricardo, so the capitalists play a crucial role in the growth process. With their investment funds, capitalists attempt to expand output by hiring more workers and purchasing additional equipment. This bids real wages above their natural level, at least for a short period. Wage increases result in a decrease in death rates and, after a lag, an increase in the work force. This, in turn, tends to drive wages down again. But, if natural resources are plentiful and profit rates high, it is possible for capital accumulation to take place so rapidly that real wages remain high for long periods.

Yet, as the population expands, poorer and poorer lands are cultivated to meet the increasing demand for food. Rents on the better grades of land rise and absorb a greater share of the output produced on these lands. This leaves less to be shared by the capitalists and workers. Profit rates decline and wages tend to fall to their natural level. As long as the profit rate is above zero, capitalists continue to accumulate and thereby keep in motion the growth of population. But, eventually the lack of fertile lands becomes an impassible barrier. This occurs when the output from a unit of labor and capital employed on the poorest land yields an output that is only sufficient to cover the natural wages of the labor involved. There is nothing left over for capital and, consequently, no incentive or means for further accumulation. The same holds true on the more fertile lands. Rents absorb the difference between the total output on these lands and the natural wages of the labor employed. The stationary state position arrives: profits are zero (or near zero); real wages are at their minimum natural levels and rents are extremely high.

The main counterforce to this pessimistic outcome is agricultural improvements which hold back the need to use the least fertile soils. Such technological progress will take place on occasion, but, in Ricardo's view, not rapidly enough to offset the eventual stationary state. Another important escape from this outcome is international trade. Industrial countries that specialize in manufactures and import cheap food from land-rich developing countries are able for a time to avoid the consequences of limited natural resources.

In a sense there is no policy a nation can follow to avoid ultimate stagnation. We might think that classical economists would have thrown up their hands in dismay over this conclusion. They never seemed to take a fatalistic view of development, however. The stationary state would, in their view, come one day, but they were always able to suggest important measures to postpone its arrival. All these policy recommendations depended upon minimum government interference. Ricardo, like other classical writers, believed that almost all taxes ultimately impinged upon profits, thereby slackening the rate of economic development. When, alternatively, capitalists were given maximum opportunity to seek profits, he believed that the invisible hand of the price mechanism would, provided monopolistic positions did not exist, efficiently allocate available resources and operate to hold back the stationary state as long as possible.

Another famous classical economist, J. S. Mill, argued that when the stationary state did eventually arrive, "it would be, on the whole, a very considerable improvement on our present condition."[5] In a vein similar to the outlook of many people today, he continues: "I confess I am not charmed with the ideal of life held out by those who think that the normal state of human beings is that of struggling to get on; that the trampling, crushing, elbowing, and treading on each other's heels, which form the existing type of social life, are the most desirable lot of human kind, or anything but the disagreeable symptoms of one of the phases of industrial progress."[6]

II. HARMONIOUS GROWTH VIA CAPITAL ACCUMULATION AND TECHNOLOGICAL PROGRESS—THE NEOCLASSICAL MODEL

What the classical economists failed, quite understandably, to foresee was the extent and persistence of the technological revolution that swept through the more developed parts of the world in the later eighteenth and nineteenth centuries. Technological progress was more than sufficient to offset the dismal consequences of diminishing returns. The crude Malthusian theory of population growth did not apply in developed countries. As income levels rose, birth rates began to decline and thus acted as a check on the rate of population increase. By the third quarter of the nineteenth century, per capita income levels in the developed countries were far above anything that could be regarded as a near-subsistence, natural level, and, moreover, were rapidly increasing. The classical theory of economic development, consequently, no longer seemed relevant for analyzing growth in the developed countries.

Most economists abandoned the simple yet sweeping approach of the classical writers. Population changes were taken as "givens" rather than being explained as part of the analysis. Likewise, technological progress was introduced as an autonomous variable determined largely by noneconomic forces. Neoclassical economists became much more "inward looking" than were their predecessors. They began to analyze the manner in which the

---

[5] J. S. Mill, *Principles of Political Economy*, London: J. W. Parker, 1888, Vol. 2, p. 308.
[6] Ibid.

price system allocated an economy's resources among the thousands of different, competing uses for them.

A. *The Process of Capital Accumulation*

One important subject that benefited significantly from this approach was capital accumulation. The classical writers took a mechanistic view of this process. Capitalists automatically reinvested most of their income as long as the profit rate was above a near-zero level. Neoclassical writers refined this analysis and made it more applicable to the institutional environment of the nineteenth and twentieth centuries.

In the neoclassical model, savers and investors need not be the same individuals. Businessmen can purchase capital goods with borrowed funds, and individuals can save by purchasing securities rather than physical assets. The capital market is the institutional arrangement whereby savers and investors are brought together, and their supply of and demand for investible funds is made consistent with each other. The price that performs this function is the interest rate. Specifically, the volume of saving is assumed to depend upon the interest rate. If the rate of interest should rise from 4 to 6%, it is assumed that individuals will save a larger fraction of a given income level. There is a very low interest-rate level at which they will consume their entire incomes, however. The supply curve of investible funds is, in other words, upward sloping like the usual supply curve. Changes in income levels also affect savings. The higher a person's income, the more he is willing to save at any given interest rate.

In neoclassical analysis the interest rate also plays a crucial role in determining investment. Businessmen compare the expected percentage yield on any investment project with the percentage rate at which they could borrow funds for it. As long as the former rate is above the latter, it is profitable to invest. In any existing state of technological knowledge, the greater the volume of investment, the lower is the yield on additional investment activities. Like the typical demand curve, the demand for investible funds, therefore, is downward sloping. However, technological improvements tend to move the entire curve to the right.

In any particular time period the intersection of the demand

and supply curves for investible funds determines both the actual market rate of interest and the volume of saving and investment. The investment undertaken adds to the economy's capital stock and thus raises the productivity of a given-size labor force. The resulting increase in national income then tends to increase the supply curve of investible funds for the next period. On the other hand, in the absence of technological progress the demand curve for investible funds drops off, since the highest yielding projects have been used up in the previous investment period. Consequently, the demand and supply curves intersect at a lower rate of interest, thereby making lower yielding projects profitable. As this process takes place, the volume of investment activity eventually declines and finally ceases when the interest rate falls to such a low level that the community as a whole does not wish to undertake net saving. This would be a stationary state position without the onus of a low per capita income level.

Most neoclassical writers optimistically refused to accept this static outcome. They agreed with Marshall's assertion: "There seems to be no good reason for believing that we are anywhere near a stationary state. . . ."[7] Their optimism was based on two important factors. First, they were confident that continued technical progress would keep opening up high yielding investment prospects. They thought that this progress would be sufficiently rapid to overcome, at least in the foreseeable future, any stagnation pressures imposed by the scarcity of natural resources. Second, they believed that any slight drop in the interest rate would make a large number of investment prospects profitable. In other words, the demand curve for investible funds was highly elastic. Consequently, it would take a long time to reach a stationary position even without technological progress.

This optimistic view presumes a willingness to save on the part of the population. If the desire to save is weak, growth will be slow no matter how favorable investment opportunities are. But neoclassical optimism extended to this area also. Although they never missed an opportunity to extol the virtues of thrift, most

---

[7] Alfred Marshall, *Principles of Economics*, London: Macmillan and Co., Ltd., 1930, 8th ed., p. 223.

neoclassical economists regarded saving to be a well-ingrained habit in the developed countries—a habit that was becoming stronger all the time.

B. *The Gradual and Harmonious Nature of Development*

Another important feature of the neoclassical view of development is the gradual and harmonious nature of growth. Unlike the Ricardian model and—even more so—the Marxian framework, neoclassical development is not a process in which one income group gains and others lose. All groups reap the benefits of growth. Technological progress may cause temporary unemployment for a particular labor group, but the net effect of such progress is to increase the demand for labor. Moreover, new methods are introduced only gradually so that in most instances even short-lived technological unemployment is not a problem.

The favorable repercussions of growth in one industry on other industries also brings out the harmonious nature of the neoclassical development process. Marshall introduced the concept of "external" economies to bring out these interrelations. By "external" economies he meant those increases in profit prospects for a particular industry which are the result of economic activity completely external to the industry. For example, as an industry expands, it requires more raw materials and services from other industries. These industries are then induced to expand. Similarly, growth may cause the price of a product such as electric power to fall owing to economies of large-scale production. This price decline in turn raises profits in industries that are important consumers of electricity. He also recognized—but did not stress—that growth in one sector could also bring external diseconomies to other sectors. The pollution problems of modern industrial economies are examples of this type of development effect. One of the great contributions of neoclassical economists was to bring out such microrelationships. They pointed out that development is not just a set of simple relations among a few general variables. Each step forward sets off a complex chain reaction that can affect many firms and industries and that itself can lead to further significant growth.

The belief that investment projects interact favorably upon one another is often used to justify support of massive, government-directed investment programs for today's developing nations. Neoclassical economists drew no such policy implications from these interrelations, however. Instead, they subscribed largely to the *laissez-faire* policy recommended by classical writers. Government intervention was needed to prevent monopolies and to provide for national defense but, in general, free atomistic competition was regarded as the most effective policy for stimulating development. They did not accept the argument that the prevalence of interrelated investment opportunities requires centralized control if the most profitable opportunities are to be fully exploited. In the neoclassical model, development occurs in small, almost continuous steps. Consequently, price is usually never very far astray as a signaling device for the most productive investment opportunities. The level of economic uncertainty is also at a minimum in such a smooth, harmonious economic environment. Investors, therefore, tend to be aware of any major interrelations that require large-scale investment and make the kind of careful cost calculations with respect to them that ensures the success of their undertaking.

III. THE CONTRADICTIONS OF CAPITALIST DEVELOPMENT—MARX

The major challenge to classical and neoclassical development theory has come from the Marxists.[8] Marx and his followers regard traditional growth theory as shallow and trivial. Conditions such as a low rate of technological progress or a lack of natural resources are, in their view, merely superficial causes of development difficulties. We must consider the nature of the economic system under which production takes place to discover the fundamental factors that fashion development. A particular economic arrangement of production determines the class structure of a society. In turn, from a specific class structure, a superstructure of ideas and institutions is formed that dominates the culture of the society. In the early stages of a new social system, the material forces of production are consistent with both the class

---

[8] Marx's major work is, of course, his three-volume work, *Capital*.

structure and the superstructure of ideas and institutions. But, the class structures and the institutions that surround them become fixed and unadaptable, whereas the material forces of production change autonomously. The existing class order becomes incompatible with the new economic forces, and a political struggle ensues between the class that would gain by social change and the class that would lose. Since the material forces of production are all-determining, the class that stands to gain always wins out eventually and brings about the establishment of a new social system.

This, then, is a thumbnail sketch of the Marxian materialistic interpretation of history. If we are to make an accurate assessment of the processes and prospects of development, we must, according to Marx, analyze growth within the framework of this theory. The particular social system about which Marx was mainly concerned was, of course, capitalism. In his view the capitalistic system contained all sorts of internal contradictions that made successful development impossible. Indeed, these contradictions were so important that the system itself eventually would collapse and be replaced by socialism. In this classless society the powerful economic forces that foster growth would be fully utilized, and the resulting development would benefit all members of society.

A. The Capitalist Model of Growth

Marx's analysis of capitalist development is as follows. There are two classes in the system: capitalists and workers. The first group owns all existing means of production (equipment and natural resources) in the economy. Workers have only their perishable labor power to sell. The goal of any capitalist is to maximize his profits (Marx lumps together rent and the return to capital under this term), not merely to raise his own living standard but, more important, to provide investment funds for the competitive race with other capitalists.

One way a capitalist can increase his earnings is by introducing cost-reducing inventions and temporarily getting a profit jump on his competitors. Opportunities for utilizing such technological improvements abound in the Marxian system. Indeed, just as the lack of adequate technological progress is the ultimate bottleneck in the classical model, the inability to cope with rapid technological progress is the underlying cause of capitalism's downfall in the Marxian model. More specifically, it is the highly labor-saving nature of technological progress that creates difficulties. Marx views technological advances under capitalism as causing mass technological unemployment. More workers are displaced directly by new machines than are absorbed via the secondary effects of lowering production costs. The resulting pool of unemployed, which Marx called "the industrial reserve army," acts as a depressing force on the wages of employed workers, and these wages fall to a subsistence level.

If there were a high degree of substitutability between machines and men, the unemployed would be gradually absorbed through the use of more labor-intensive methods of production. But Marx postulates a fixed relation between equipment and labor for any given technological state. At any one time the stock of capital is not large enough to utilize all available labor. Moreover, as capitalists seek to increase their rate of capital accumulation by introducing new productive methods, the situation becomes worse since, on balance, the new techniques increase unemployment. Thus, more and more of the working class is thrown into the industrial reserve army, and wages for those lucky enough to hold jobs are driven to minimum levels.

The capitalists fare little better, according to Marx. They become increasingly caught up in a competitive battle where ruthlessness is a prerequisite for survival. For example, in an attempt to avoid being swallowed up by other firms, each capitalist tries to maintain his profit rate by lengthening the work day and reducing wages below even subsistence levels. Hiring of women and children at such low wages is another way to maintain high profits. Yet, even with these forms of exploitation, many capitalists fail and are driven into the working class. Fewer and fewer capitalists assume control over larger and larger amounts of capital.

The widening gap between capitalists and workers leads to successively deeper cyclical crises that lower the profits of even the strongest capitalists. A major cause of such crises is underconsumption. The consuming power of the workers is limited by their poverty, whereas that of the capitalists is restricted by their need to save in order to survive in the competitive struggle. Consequently, a general glut occurs periodically when consumption falls short of the producing powers of the economy.

One of the most significant features about Marx's description of capitalist development was his insistence that the nature of economic activities in colonial areas depended upon what was taking place in the developed, capitalistic countries. He argued, for example, that "the discovery of gold and silver in America, the extirpation, enslavement and entombment in mines of the aboriginal population, the beginning of the conquest and looting of the East Indies, the turning of Africa into a warren for the commercial hunting of black-skins" provided a major source of capital for the developed countries.[9] Likewise, the same colonial areas served as important markets for the mass-produced manufactures of the developed nations.

As the development process becomes more unstable and vicious within the advanced capitalistic countries, these countries impose tighter and tighter controls over their colonies. Every effort is made to develop cheap sources of raw materials and foodstuffs in these countries and to discourage the establishment of competing manufacturing activities. Wage rates in mines and on plantations, for example, are deliberately kept low by monopolistic actions, and traditional handicraft industries are destroyed by the flood of cheap manufactures from the developed countries. The net outcome is that the less developed, colonial areas do not benefit from capitalist development. Their traditional economies are destroyed and replaced by an unbalanced economic structure that exists only for exploitation by desperate capitalistic countries, which are trying to avoid economic stagnation and political revolution.

B. Conclusions

It has been over a hundred years since Marx first predicted the downfall of capitalism, and the cry "wait till next year" has long since become empty and meaningless. Yet, within the less developed parts of today's world, Karl Marx remains one of the most

---

[9] Karl Marx, *Capital*, Chicago: Charles H. Kerr and Co., 1926, Vol. I, p. 823.

respected and widely read of all economists. The reasons for his popularity are not easy to comprehend. But his handling of development issues seems to strike many people in less developed countries as coming from someone who "really understands our problems." Perhaps this is mainly because, until comparatively recent years, there were no satisfactory alternatives between the overly simple growth theories of classical and neoclassical writers and the Marxian approach, which is more sympathetic than substantial.

For, in terms of hard economic reasons, there is little that is solid in the Marxian system. His basic principle concerning the perverse nature of technological progress has more than a hundred years of experience against it. Technological unemployment has been an occasional problem, but it has by no means occurred on a mass scale. Similarly, in the developed countries wages are far above the subsistence level Marx seemed to be talking about. Moreover, workers seem to be sharing in the benefits of growth in developing countries where capitalism is strong. Also, the so-called "law" concerning the concentration of capital has not held up. The absolute size of firms has, of course, grown tremendously in all countries, but in the United States, for example, there does not appear to have been any significant change in the degree of business concentration from the turn of the century to the present period. The Marxian analysis of business cycles is likewise inadequate. Like many other writers he was dissatisfied with the notion that there could never be a chronic deficiency in effective demand. His discussion of the matter, however, is more of an assertion of its possibility than an explanation as to why it could occur. In short, Marx fails to make a good case for the explosive nature of capitalist development. His works are full of insights into the nature of the growth process, but he does not build a logically sound theory of economic development.

3

Modifications to Traditional Development Theory

This chapter continues analyzing the manner in which capital accumulation brings about economic development by introducing some of the main, pre-World War II modifications to the traditional explanations set forth in the preceding chapter. Specifically, the contributions of Schumpeter, Keynes, and the post-Keynesians toward understanding the process of economic development will be considered. Schumpeter, who is perhaps less well-known than most of the writers discussed in Chapters 2 and 3, is studied because of his outstanding contribution in emphasizing the role of the entrepreneur in leading the accumulation process. Keynes and other stagnationists of the 1930's are important because of their integration of a much-improved theory of aggregate demand with existing development theory. However, the integration was only partial. It remained for the post-Keynesian economists to complete the task of bringing together both the demand-creating and supply-creating effects of capital accumulation.

I. THE ENTREPRENEUR AND DISHARMONIOUS GROWTH—SCHUMPETER

One outstanding economist who attempted to bridge the gap between Marxian and neoclassical development was Joseph

Schumpeter.[1] Schumpeter was dissatisfied with the neoclassical view that development was a gradual and harmonious process. Some growth occurs smoothly, but not, according to Schumpeter, the growth that sparks significant breakthroughs to higher living standards. Economic changes of this sort occur in leaps and spurts as vast new investment opportunities open up; for example, the growth of railroads in the nineteenth century and electrification and automotive expansion in this century. Such major economic spurts also create business cycles in developing economies. Indeed, Schumpeter believed that long-run growth could only be understood when considered in a cyclical context.

This vision of the way development takes place is very similar to Marx's in stressing the dynamic, uneven nature of economic growth. But Marx's influence on Schumpeter stopped there. He rejected Marx's economic concepts as well as the conclusions Marx tried to reach with them. Instead, Schumpeter used the tools and concepts fashioned by neoclassical economists. He was particularly impressed by the general-equilibrium approach of the more mathematical neoclassical writers.

A. The Entrepreneur and His Role

Once economic development is viewed as often occurring in leaps and spurts, the neoclassical theory of capital accumulation looks more and more unsatisfactory. In an economy in which growth takes place in an uneven fashion, major business decisions involve a high degree of risk and uncertainty. The neoclassical picture of businessmen carefully comparing expected yields with the interest rate may not be relevant in these circumstances. The margin of possible error in one's estimate of expected yield from an investment project may be so high that the particular interest-rate level is unimportant in determining the volume of investment. If it is highly uncertain whether a firm can earn 10 or 20% on a capital project, then whether the cost of funds is 6 or 5% is not likely to be crucial in the investment decision.

Schumpeter visualized that most major investments that lead

---

[1] J. A. Schumpeter's main work relating to economic development is: *The Theory of Economic Development,* Cambridge: Harvard University Press, 1934.

the economy forward are made under such conditions. Ordinary businessmen hesitate to invest in such an environment. It takes a special sort of person, the entrepreneur, to get things moving. The entrepreneur is motivated by much more than the standard desire to raise his income level. He has such grandiose goals as conquering others in competitive economic battles, the desire to establish a private dynasty, and the wish to create something entirely new. His drives are so strong that he is willing to undertake investment activity in a highly dynamic economy while the person with ordinary motivations will not.

So entrepreneurship is the key to economic development in the Schumpeterian system. The entrepreneur's role is to innovate; to undertake new combinations of productive factors. He may introduce a new commodity into the market, utilize a new productive method, open up a new market area, develop a new source of raw-material supply, or completely reorganize an existing industry. The entrepreneur is neither an inventor nor a capitalist who furnishes investible funds, although a particular entrepreneur might also fulfill these roles. The essence of entrepreneurship is creating something new *in the market place*. There is, so Schumpeter believed, never any lack of technological improvements. What is sometimes absent is the entrepreneurial talent needed to introduce these inventions into the economy. Thus, the most crucial person in the development process is the one who directs the use of investment funds, not the one who furnishes these funds.

B. Development Via Inflation

Schumpeter went even further in playing down the role of the individual who voluntarily and deliberately saves part of his income. In his model, entrepreneurs obtain the funds they need to finance their innovations from credit-creating banks. These banks merely create new money on the basis of the fractional reserve system and then lend it to entrepreneurs.

This inflationary policy leads to an increase in real investment in the following manner. Assume that the economy is stationary with full employment but no net investment. New profit opportunities exist, however, and, if entrepreneurs are present, they will begin to exploit them. A few entrepreneurs initiate investment activity by borrowing from commercial banks. With these funds they are able to bid away the factors of production they need for their capital projects from the consumption-goods industries in which they are being used. The shift of these factors curtails the output of consumption goods and, in a sense, forces the economy to save more, that is, consume less in real terms. What happens in the market place is that prices of consumer goods go up faster than the money incomes of most people, and so the quantity of consumer goods obtained with these incomes declines.

Soon many entrepreneurs begin investment activity with additional innovational plans. Prices and money incomes begin to increase throughout the economy. Now borrowing no longer is confined to innovational activities. The expectation of rising prices and lagging costs encourages ordinary businessmen to expand investment under existing methods of production. Before long, however, the flow of goods from the initial entrepreneurial undertakings begins to have a significant effect on economic activity. Schumpeter called this effect the process of creative destruction. New products and methods begin to replace old commodities and techniques. Firms engaged in producing these traditional items are forced into positions requiring either costly readjustments or even bankruptcy. The early entrepreneurs, meanwhile, are repaying their bank loans out of profits made from their innovations.

These latter two factors, the destruction caused by innovations and the deflation associated with loan repayments, bring the investment boom to an end. The uncertainty caused by the process of creative destruction becomes so great that even entrepreneurial investment activity ceases. As this happens and bank repayments become more significant, the investment program based on existing techniques collapses. Its only basis for existence was rising prices, and investment quickly decreases once the rate of inflation begins to decline. Not only does the boom come to an end, but a depression generally occurs when the decline in economic activity overshoots its stationary equilibrium point. But this depression phase of the business cycle is, according to Schumpeter, usually short-lived. The economy automatically tends to return to a full-employment position. The stage is then set for another wave of innovations.

On narrow economic grounds Schumpeter could see no reason for economic development of the kind just described ever coming to an end. It was uneven and disharmonious to a certain extent, but not enough to upset the free-market capitalist system. The benefits, in terms of increases in the quantity and quality of goods made available to all income groups, more than offset the costs of uneven growth.

Schumpeter, nonetheless, was pessimistic about capitalism's future. First, he thought he saw innovation turning from an individual activity into a routinized, depersonalized activity undertaken within the bureaucracy of big business. Next, he felt that the growth of the giant business corporation, in which control was frequently separated from ownership, was weakening the fundamental capitalist institutions of private property and freedom of contract. Finally, Schumpeter was concerned about the ability of businessmen and industrialists to hold their leadership in capitalistic governments. He was afraid that they would not keep the allegiance of labor, and socialism would eventually emerge. He saw no reason for the rate of economic development to be any less under this system, however.

C. Appraisal

Schumpeter's great contribution to development theory was his emphasis on the importance of the entrepreneurial function. He recognized that development was more than putting money into the bank and watching it grow. Development involves significant change, and there must be individuals who can lead a process of basic economic change. Schumpeter had little to say about why some countries seem to possess more entrepreneurial talent than others. His only observations on that subject were that entrepreneurs are not a class in the same sense that capitalists and workers are, and that capitalism is a favorable environment in which entrepreneurship can flourish.

Another significant contribution of Schumpeter was his analysis of development via inflationary financing. It is a method that almost every government of a developing country tries to use at one time or another. Most present-day economists would say that Schumpeter underestimated the difficulties of increasing investment by this means over a long period. Its success depends upon the existence of a money illusion. Individuals, whose money income level has remained constant, must continue to spend the same amount in the same manner, even though their real income level has declined because of a price-level increase. But, should these individuals wish to purchase a certain quantity of goods in real terms, they would respond to general price rises by borrowing or by drawing on their cash stocks. If everyone behaves in this way, it will be impossible for entrepreneurs to obtain investment resources even temporarily. People may be fooled for a short time by a money illusion, but not for long. More will be said on this point in Chapter 8.

Schumpeter's predictions about the end of capitalism have few supporters. His points demonstrate that capitalism has changed considerably since the eighteenth century. Even granting their validity does not lead to the conclusion that socialism will eventually emerge. It simply means that capitalism has changed and may keep changing.

II. THE STAGNATIONISTS AND THE POST-KEYNESIAN GROWTH THEORISTS

In classical and neoclassical economics the possibility of long-run mass unemployment does not exist. Almost all writers in the classical tradition granted that short periods of general unemployment were possible during deep economic crises, but they believed there were powerful forces that ensured full employment in the long run. Consequently they introduced assumptions into their aggregative analysis that prevented the possibility of less than full employment.

Marx and a few other economists unsuccessfully challenged the empirical validity of these assumed relationships. It was not until the depression of the 1930's had dragged along for several years that economists became highly critical of neoclassical employment theory. Finally, in 1936, J. M. Keynes produced a new theory of employment that revolutionized aggregative economics.[2] The standard elementary textbook analysis of national income determination, which now is such an important part of most beginning courses, is based on the work of this English economist.

A. *Keynesian Employment Theory*

In the Keynesian theory of national-income determination, the level of investment depends upon the same factors as in the neoclassical model, namely, the rates of return or yields of successive increments of investment and the rate of interest. Specifically, businessmen continue to undertake new investment projects as long as the percentage rate of return from the marginal project is higher than the interest rate. A drop in the interest rate or a general increase in the profitability of investment projects due to a factor such as technological progress will encourage additional investment. The level of saving in the Keynesian system is, on the other hand, not determined in quite the same way as in the neoclassical model. Keynes made saving (and consumption) a function of only the level of income, whereas neoclassical writers stressed both income and the interest rate, especially the latter, as determinants of saving (consumption).

Taking as given the market rate of interest and assuming a particular investment-demand schedule, we can first determine the volume of investment that business firms will undertake. Given this investment and a particular saving (and consumption) function, the equilibrium level of national income is then determined via the familiar multiplier process. According to Keynes, this income level may not be high enough to provide full employment for the available labor force.

Prior to Keynesian employment theory it was generally argued that any tendency for a less-than-full employment situation could be corrected if the government expanded the money supply sufficiently. With a greater money supply, lenders would be willing to make loans at lower interest rates, which then would increase the volume of investment and level of income in the economy.

---

[2] J. M. Keynes, *The General Theory of Employment, Interest and Money,* New York: Harcourt, Brace and Co., 1936.

Keynes claimed, however, that if unemployment existed when interest rates were already low, monetary policy might be ineffective in increasing employment. Potential lenders of funds might prefer simply to hoard any increased holdings of money because the small return earned from making additional loans would be insufficient to offset the risks involved in lending.

Keynes and many other economists of the 1930's thought that unemployment would persist as a long-run problem unless governments played a greater role in the economy. Their main basis for this conclusion was a pessimistic outlook concerning future investment opportunities. They could not see any technological improvements on the investment horizon comparable to the great discoveries of the nineteenth and early twentieth centuries. There also seemed to be few rich geographic areas left to develop, and even the investment demand provided by a rapidly growing population was dropping. In their view the outcome could in some ways be worse than the classical stationary state position. At least in the stationary position everyone was employed. But, in a world where less than full-employment equilibrium is possible, a lack of adequate growth and mass unemployment go together.

The main policy proposed by Keynes to counteract the dismal prospects for private investment was government spending covered by deficit financing. This spending would, directly and indirectly through the multiplier process, increase aggregate demand and restore national income to its full-employment level. Moreover, since available resources are underutilized, this increase in aggregate spending can be accomplished without inflation.

Although Keynes directed his analysis at developed economies, his policy recommendation has had considerable appeal in less developed countries. These countries, too, suffer from widespread unemployment. Consequently, is not a deficit-financed government investment program the easy, painless solution to the development and employment goals of these countries? Unfortunately, unemployment, though extensive, is usually confined to unskilled workers. In addition, excess capacity prevails only in particular industries and sectors. Because of shortages and bottlenecks elsewhere, deficit financing is most likely to result in a rise in the price level without any increase in real output.

B. Post-Keynesian Growth Theory

Keynesian economics focuses upon the aggregate demand-creating effects of investment. Little is said in this analysis about the fact that investment also increases the aggregate-output capacity of the economy. Keynes was mainly interested in the problem of utilizing fully the labor and capital stock already available and, quite understandably, abstracted from the capacity-creating effects of investment. It remained for the so-called post-Keynesian growth theorists to incorporate these effects into the Keynesian model.[3] These economists, like Keynes, were concerned primarily with the growth problems of developed countries. However, the simple growth model they built has been widely used in developing economies, both for forecasting development rates and for specifying the saving requirements of particular per capita income growth targets.

A given level of real income is maintained in the simple Keynesian system as long as investment remains at a fixed level. If the investment level increases, equilibrium income rises by some multiple of the increase in investment. This multiple depends upon the shape of the saving or consumption function. The increase in aggregate demand will equal the increase in investment, ΔI, multiplied by the reciprocal of the marginal propensity (assumed to be equal to the average propensity) to save, $1/s$.

Investment (in a net sense) also adds to the economy's capital stock and thus to its productive capacity. It is not merely the increment in investment over previous periods that does this, but the total net investment each period. If a given increase in the economy's capital stock (together with appropriate increases in other factors of production) always increases the economy's po-

---

[3] The two individuals who did the most in developing post-Keynesian growth theory are R. Harrod and E. Domar. See R. Harrod, *Towards a Dynamic Economics*, London: Macmillan and Co., Ltd., 1948; and E. Domar, "Expansion and Employment," *American Economic Review*, **37**, pp. 34–35 (March 1947).

tential output by a fixed amount, then the reciprocal of this incremental capital-output ratio, $1/k$, multiplied by the actual volume of investment, I, equals the increase in the economy's capacity or potential output.

In order to fully employ the labor force and capital stock without deflationary or inflationary pressures, any increases in the economy's aggregate-supply capacity must be matched by an equivalent increment in aggregate demand. In terms of the concepts just outlined, the equilibrium condition for full-employment growth is: $\Delta I/s = I/k$. This can be arranged into: $\Delta I/I = s/k$. The relationship states that investment must grow at some constant rate (s/k), if full employment growth without inflation or deflation is to be maintained. Real income will also grow at this rate. With an incremental capital-output ratio of 3 ($1/k$ is then 1/3) and a marginal propensity to save of 1/10, the equilibrium growth rate is: $1/3 \times 1/10 = 1/30$ or 3.3%.

Some post-Keynesian economists used this relationship to emphasize that there were grounds for being even more pessimistic than Keynes about future growth prospects. It was not just enough to achieve a high-investment level to avoid stagnation. The absolute level of investment must become larger and larger each period in order to avoid this outcome. This made the problem of declining investment opportunities even more serious. Other writers stressed the cyclical implications of the theory by pointing out the difficulty of achieving precisely the proper rate of investment for steady growth. Once the economy departs from the equilibrium growth rate, moreover, it is likely to be driven still further away from it.

The manner in which the simple post-Keynesian growth equation is often applied to forecasting and planning in developing countries is as follows. Suppose a government sets as its target growth rate a 2% annual increase in per capita income. Assume, further, that it is necessary to increase the economy's stock of capital goods by $3 in order to increase output by $1 annually. The incremental capital-output ratio, in other words, is 3. Suppose also that the population is expected to grow at an annual rate of 2.5%. With this information, planners can now determine how much saving and investing their country must undertake in order to achieve the target growth rate. Since the population will grow at a 2.5% rate it will be necessary to increase the total output at the same rate just to maintain the per capita income. To obtain a 2% increase in per capita income, the total output must rise at approximately 4.5% (2% + 2½%) annually. Because $3 worth of investment is needed for each $1 worth of additional output, the economy must therefore save and invest 13.5% (3 × 4.5%) of its national product each year to attain its target growth rate.

This estimating technique would seem to be an extremely simple method for answering one of the most important questions facing development planners, namely: How much investment is required to achieve the target increase in per capita income? Alternatively, the actual growth rate of per capita income can be roughly estimated by dividing the actual saving ratio by the incremental capital-output ratio and then subtracting the predicted growth rate for population. There are, however, serious limitations to the use of capital-output ratios for predictive purposes. Increases in output are a result not only of capital accumulation but also of quantitative and qualitative changes in natural resources, the labor force, and technology. Predicting on the basis of a constant capital-output ratio assumes that these factors will continue to bear the same relationship to increments in the capital stock that they did in the period used for calculating the capital-output ratio. There is certainly no reason to expect this to hold, especially if the rate of capital accumulation is being increased under the development plan. The structure of production also changes considerably as development efforts proceed. Since historical capital-output ratios vary widely among different industries, quite inaccurate results can be obtained by using past capital-output ratios for the economy, as a whole, in predicting future growth. Moreover, in order to determine the most socially beneficial pattern of production to undertake as development takes place, it is necessary to take account of labor and raw-material costs as well as capital costs. Consequently, historical capital-output ratios for individual industries are of little use in trying to estimate future saving and investment requirements.

These conceptual drawbacks to the use of capital-output ratios plus the many statistical problems connected with obtaining accurate measures of these magnitudes lead to the conclusion that simple planning calculations based on these ratios must be regarded as very rough. We would almost like to say they are worthless and should not be used at all. However, such is the state of statistical information in most developing countries in relation to the planning efforts they are making that this would be going too far. It is often a matter of employing this technique as a first rough approximation of investment requirements or using even cruder rules of thumb. But the limitations and drawbacks of this predictive method should always be remembered.

4

Recent Contributions to Development Theory (I)

The growth theories outlined in the last two chapters until recently represented the main body of existing analysis on economic development. Since World War II, however, there has been a great spurt of interest in this subject. A number of analysts have attempted to adapt the great development theories to particular conditions of today's developing countries. But several new and important contributions have also been made toward a better understanding of the processes and obstacles of economic development. In the next two chapters some of these recent contributions will be discussed.

The present chapter focuses upon modern analyses directed at explaining why underdeveloped countries failed to grow very rapidly despite their exposure years ago to greatly improved technology as well as to external aid in the form of foreign capital and entrepreneurship. As pointed out previously, up to the post-World War II period the only major explanation as to why foreign investment in the less developed countries failed to touch off the kind of self-generating growth described by neoclassical writers was that put forth by Marx. However, in recent years much of the development analysis has been directed at explaining why self-sustaining growth failed to catch on. Three strands of thinking along these lines are considered in this chapter. The first combines the Ricardian relationship between population growth and per capita income with the post-Keynesian relationship between the rate of growth of output and per capita income levels and shows how an economy can become enmeshed in a "population trap." The next section develops the notion that some export industries on which less developed countries initially specialized did not produce secondary effects that were favorable for stimulating further development. Finally, the chapter considers certain arguments that put the blame for low rates of growth upon foreign monopoly and an unfavorable long-run trend in the ratio of export to import prices for the less developed countries.

I. THE POPULATION TRAP

Recent writers agree that the tremendous population surge that seems to follow any increase in per capita income is a major barrier to rising living standards. Not only do these population increases slow down the growth of per capita income simply because any increase in total income must be shared by more people, but also they may diminish the rate of growth of total income. This latter effect is due to the decline in total saving (and investment) that tends to occur at any income level when this income is distributed among a greater number of people. Some economies seem to take a few steps forward in per capita income terms only to be met by such an explosion in population that living standards are in danger of being driven back to or even below their initial levels.

The notion of such a "population trap" is illustrated by the following diagram (Figure 4.1). The curve *PP′* indicates the relationship that exists between the level of per capita income and the rate of population growth. At very low per capita income levels, health and nutritional levels decline until the mortality rate exceeds the birth rate. Conversely, as per capita income rises, the death rate declines sharply, and population expands at a faster and faster rate until its upper limit of around 3% is reached. The curve is drawn to turn down finally at very high per capita income levels because of a decline in the birth rate.

The curve *YY′* is based on the relation between the saving ratio, the capital-output ratio, and the growth rate of total in-

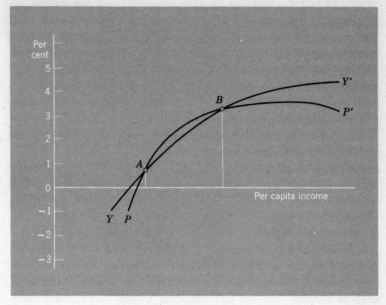

Figure 4-1. The population trap.

come. As the post-Keynesian model shows, given a fixed capital-output ratio, the rate of income growth increases as the saving ratio increases. Since the saving ratio is assumed to be a function of per capita income, the curve rises from a zero growth rate at a low per capita income figure to some maximum growth rate at higher per capita income levels where the saving ratio reaches an upper limit.

Point *A* on the diagram illustrates the population trap. If per capita income level is raised a small amount beyond the level corresponding to *A*, the increase in saving will act to raise the rate of income expansion but the decline in death rate will increase the rate of population growth even more. Per capita income, therefore, will be driven back to the level corresponding to point *A*, at which income and population grow at the same rate. However, per capita income also cannot fall below this level for long. At levels just to the left of *A*, the rate of population increase is less than the rate of increase in the economy's income. Point *A* is, therefore, a position of stable equilibrium. At per capita income levels somewhat above and below it, income and population pressure operate to drive per capita income back to this point.

However, consider per capita income levels to the right of *B*. At these levels the forces making for higher per capita income levels are greater than those tending to depress it. The economy has then reached a position at which self-sustaining growth occurs.

The policy implications of this diagrammatic analysis are obvious. Unless major efforts are made to lift per capita income, the developing economies will not succeed in raising per capita income levels more than temporarily. Foreign aid and domestic measures aimed at raising the internal-saving ratio move the *YY'* curve upward and to the left. Similarly, effects directed towards reducing birth rates shift the *PP'* curve downward. Should the income and population curves no longer intersect beyond the existing per capita income level, the economy is on the path of cumulative growth. If per capita income should reach levels to the right of *B*, it would thus be possible to cut back on programs such as foreign aid and still maintain an upward trend in per capita income.

Of course, just how the income and population curves look for any particular country is an empirical question that is not easy to answer. Certainly, except for a few developing nations forced with unusual political problems, total income is growing faster than population. It is also evident, however, that we can be a good deal more certain about continued high rates of population growth than about continued high rates of income growth. Consequently, although no country presently seems to be in the low-level equilibrium of the population trap, this analysis is useful for focusing upon the strong downward pressures operating on per capita income in developing countries.

II. THE ROLE OF NATURAL
RESOURCES AND TECHNOLOGY

One significant feature of recent development theory is its disaggregative nature. Economists have found that the development process can be better understood if the economy is divided into broad sectors, such as the rural subsistence sector, the export sector, and the domestic industrial sector, and the economic interactions among these sectors are then analyzed. Similarly, in explaining past development patterns, students of development now place considerable emphasis upon differences among developing countries in such matters as natural-resource endowments and the nature of the export commodity upon which they initially specialized. Simple, aggregative analyses that are supposed to apply to all developing countries have not proved very useful.

Consider the pattern of development that has emerged in many mineral-exporting countries. The dualistic nature of underdeveloped economies is particularly evident within these countries. One part of the economy employs advanced productive techniques with complex capital equipment and highly skilled labor while another part uses backward inefficient methods. In the first sector—the modern, monetary part of the economy—an elaborate system of specialization and exchange exists. In the other part—the rural subsistence sector—individual families and villages produce most of the output they consume, and monetary exchange with other parts of the economy is only a small part of economic activity.

The modern, monetary sectors of these economies were developed under the impetus of foreign investment and foreign entrepreneurial activity. Local resources were not much more than sufficient to keep these economies stationary at a comparatively low-income level. But foreign investors were able to combine profitably the large markets for mineral products in developed countries and the rich supplies of these products in less developed countries. Very large capital outlays were required, however, not only for obtaining and processing the minerals themselves, but also for developing railroads, harbor and dock facilities, financial services, and storage facilities.

According to neoclassical development theory, we might expect that this foreign investment and the associated international trade would touch off a cumulative-development sequence resulting finally in a position where all parts of the economy were growing on a self-sustained basis. No such outcome has occurred, of course. Instead, outside investment has often seemed to result in the establishment of "enclave economies." Productive activities are highly advanced in these export enclaves, but they are small and have little impact on the rest of the economy.

One recent line of development thinking stresses the significance of the productive techniques employed in the new export sector as a factor that influenced the pattern of development in less developed countries. Mineral production, such as oil, copper, and bauxite, generally tends for technological reasons to require a comparatively high ratio of capital to labor. Substitution of labor for capital is, of course, possible and occurs in response to changes in factor prices, but the extent of the substitution that is profitable over wide shifts in relative factor prices is quite limited. In other words, crude-oil production, for example, tends to be organized on a highly capital intensive basis whether or not unskilled labor is inexpensive compared to capital costs. Furthermore, the complex capital equipment needed for mineral production requires complicated machinery and highly skilled labor. The newly developing nations which opened up for mineral exportation were not able to produce these items efficiently themselves. Foreign investment funds went largely to purchase capital equipment in the developed countries. It was likewise cheaper to purchase many of the current inputs into mineral production, for example, explosives, from developed countries rather than establishing input suppliers within the developing countries.

This meant that the direct and indirect economic impact of the mineral industry on the rest of the economy was slight. Comparatively few workers were employed, and even the more skilled of these were brought in from developed countries. Expansion largely took the form of increasing the stock of imported capital goods. The large profits made were either returned to the developed countries or invested in further export expansion. The lack of a large domestic market and of an adequate supply of skilled labor did not make it profitable for foreign investors to direct their activities toward internal markets.

There was, however, in many areas an important demographic repercussion related to foreign-investment activity. This was the rapid population expansion touched off by the spread of public-health measures and techniques imported from the developed countries. In many cases political control accompanied foreign investment, and health and medical advances spread through colonial administrative channels. These advances sharply reduced death rates and increased the labor force. The export sector, because of its highly capital-intensive nature, was able to absorb only a small portion of the new workers. The others were forced to seek their livelihood in the rural-subsistence sector. Productive possibilities in this sector did not tend to be fixed or capital intensive. However, the additional labor could only be absorbed by increasing the ratio of labor to land, since the rate of capital accumulation was very low. In some developing areas where land was relatively scarce, the productivity of labor in the rural sector fell to such low levels that the labor force was fully utilized for only a few months each year. Thus, in some mineral economies, underemployment and surplus labor conditions were the eventual outcome of foreign investment and export growth.

Two other types of developing countries where natural resources and technology played an important but different role in fashioning development are export economies based on plantation production and on peasant production. Agricultural production where the large-scale plantation system is usually the most efficient productive organization, such as for tea, tobacco, and coffee production, tends to be highly labor-intensive compared to mineral production. Not only are labor requirements absolutely high for plantation products, but only modest skills are needed. Export specialization based on a plantation commodity in a sense fits both natural resource-endowment and labor-endowment conditions in the underdeveloped countries. Mineral exploitation, on the other hand, is based largely upon the existence of favorable natural resources.

Because labor requirements for the typical plantation commodity are high, the direct employment effects from expanding exports as well as the secondary repercussions based on the spending of the labor force tend to be relatively large. Many of the capital goods needed to produce labor-intensive, plantation products also could be efficiently produced domestically with the aid of local, simply trained labor. Although the demand for labor was large, so too was the supply response of population to the mortality reducing measures of colonial administrators.

In many areas where land was plentiful, export growth involved the use of previously uncultivated land and the utilization of labor drawn from the existing pool in the subsistence sector, from new workers, and even, in some instances, from workers from other countries. A larger proportion of the economy tended to be drawn into the monetary export sector, but, by and large, resources were sufficiently plentiful to prevent any upward pressures on wages. More and more of the economy became involved in export production, but there were few cost-induced changes in productive methods.

There were also few opportunities for the labor force to acquire new skills. Most of the tasks in plantation production were simple. Workers came to their jobs without any labor skills, and they left with few more. Mineral production, in contrast, generally involved a wide range of labor skills. In time an unskilled worker could acquire labor skills that not only made him more valuable to the export industry but also to manufacturing activities in general. The export industry acted as a training school that gradually tended to create an industrial-labor force. Unfortunately, this labor-training impact was too small to set off sustained growth. In the plantation economy, on the other hand, the immediate labor-employing impact of export development tended to be large, but there were few additional effects insofar as improving the quality of the labor force was concerned. Thus, the economy tended to be blocked from further diversification of its productive structure.

The peasant export economy represents another special case where natural-resource conditions and technology combined to create a particular pattern of development. When these economies were opened up, production of exports such as rice and cocoa on small family-size farms was already taking place or was very easily introduced into existing family farms. Moreover, there was a considerable degree of unemployed or surplus labor on these productive units due to the lack of local markets to absorb all that could be produced. There was not only a surplus of labor but also of fertile land. All that was needed to initiate rapid development was to establish a modern transportation system and to exploit world markets. This was the function that foreign investors and entrepreneurs fulfilled so well.

Similar to the development in the plantation economy, growth in the peasant economy tended to be more horizontal than vertical. With plentiful land and an abundant labor supply, maintained by the same population spurt that affected the other two economies, export production expanded rapidly by utilizing existing peasant farms more fully and by increasing their number. Little in the way of introducing more productive techniques or increasing farm size occurred during this period of rapid export production. When it was all over and there was no more surplus land or surplus labor, these economies found themselves larger but with an unchanged productive structure. Yet conditions were not quite the same. Population pressures continued to build up, without any convenient outlet, in the form of plentiful supplies of rich land. The only way to maintain or increase per capita income was by introducing better productive techniques and more capital. Some of the peasant economies of Southeast Asia and Africa now find themselves at this point.

III. UNFAVORABLE TERMS OF TRADE AND FOREIGN MONOPOLY

Probably the explanation most widely held by non-Marxian economists as to why growth in developing countries has not been more rapid in the past is based upon certain unfavorable market forces. Some economists from these countries claim, for example, that the developed countries have exercised their monopoly powers to bring about a significant long-run decline in the terms of trade with them. Their argument goes as follows. In recession periods the large-scale, monopolistic manufactures typical of developed countries reduced production rather than prices. In prosperous periods they not only increased output but also raised wages and thus prices under the bargaining pressures of well-organized labor unions. Unfortunately, neither producers nor workers in the developing countries usually possessed sufficient monopoly power to influence the world prices of their products. In direct response to world-demand conditions, the prices of their primary products fell in recession periods and rose again in the prosperity phase of the international-business cycle. The net long-run result has been an increase in the prices of manufactured items (the imports of the developing countries) relative to the prices of primary products (the exports of these countries). This, in turn, has meant that the developing countries were able to purchase fewer and fewer capital goods with a given quantity of primary-product exports. Had this decline in purchasing power not occurred, development would have spread from the export sector throughout the rest of the developing economies.

A similar argument points to the domination of the export and import sectors in less developed countries by foreign-owned enterprises, which used their monopoly positions in a way that held back growth in these countries. Foreign-owned trading firms, for example, charged higher than competitive prices for the imported consumer goods they sold to the indigenous people. At the same time, they purchased the export commodities supplied by peasant producers at monopsonistic prices. In cases where mines and plantations were directly owned by foreigners, monopsonistic power was exerted by paying local workers less than the competitive wage level. These actions reduced local-spending power, curtailing the stimulating effects that local purchasers have on growth. The enlarged profits made by foreign firms were not even plowed back into the developing countries, but went back to the developed countries. In short, the potential for additional growth existed as developing nations expanded their exports, but this growth potential was never realized because of monopolistic actions by foreign investors.

It is difficult to assess the significance of the terms-of-trade and monopolistic-exploitation arguments. The terms-of-trade argument is on shaky grounds both empirically and theoretically. The long-run data on export and import prices for the developing nations are not sufficiently comprehensive nor accurate enough for us to be sure about actual price behavior. The best work on the subject does suggest, however, that the terms of trade did decline for the developing countries between 1900 and 1952. However, as noted in Chapter 1, there has been no significant trend either upward or downward in their trading terms since the mid-century point. But, a serious drawback of any long-run measure of changes in the terms of trade is the inability to account adequately for quality improvements in the traded items. There is little doubt that the manufactured goods imported into the developing countries have improved much more over the last 70 years than has the quality of the primary products exported from these countries. Perhaps this factor has more than offset the 33% terms-of-trade decline that one writer found in the first half of the century for the developing countries.

The monopoly explanation of the long-run terms-of-trade decline is a theoretical possibility, but more detailed supporting evidence is necessary before it can be accepted with much confidence. It is by no means clear that the developed countries have exerted greater monopoly pressures on international prices than the developing countries, especially in recent years. Furthermore, the monopoly effects of extensive, well-organized trade unions may actually operate to hold down prices in the long-run below what they would be in competitive markets because of the lags involved in collective bargaining on a national basis.

Actually, the difficulty that developing countries have had in maintaining their terms of trade would seem to be explainable on more straightforward grounds than the monopoly argument. The inflexibility of resources in these countries works against them in regard to their trading terms. When a developing country happens to specialize in a commodity whose production is highly profitable, it is likely to be a fairly short-lived situation since new competitors soon enter the field. Investors in developed countries quickly develop additional supplies in other developing countries. On the other hand, once this market declines and the product's price falls, resources in the developing countries do not move quickly out of this productive line. Compared to what happens in developed countries when markets decline, capital and labor remain tied up in the market and act to keep the price of the product from rising again to a profitable level. Given the ever-changing conditions of world demand, the less developed nations always tend to find themselves overly committed in declining industries. A decline in their terms of trade can easily occur.

Unfortunately, tariff policies of the developed countries have not helped in moving the resources of the developing economies into some of the most rapidly expanding commodity lines. The industrial countries have traditionally imposed very low or no tariffs on imports of raw materials but have highly protected the processing activities associated with manufacturing. This has discouraged the developing country from producing manufactures for export and thereby being better able to supply their own small markets by taking advantage of the economies of large-scale production.

Most economists seem to agree that prior to the postwar period and the political-independence movement in the developing countries there was some validity to the monopolistic-exploitation argument. Granting that foreign enterprises were able to make monopoly profits is, however, quite different from stating that growth would have been faster in the developing countries in the absence of these profits. Perhaps, without the prospects of these high profits, foreign investors would not have underwritten the investment cost of growth in the developing nations. Moreover, even if these profits had not been made by foreign firms, we cannot be sure that growth would have spread more extensively throughout the underdeveloped countries. Shortages of labor skills and of capital would also have had to be overcome.

In recent years the monopoly power of foreign firms seems to have diminished considerably. Government purchasing schemes have, for example, increasingly replaced private trading companies as the market contact for peasant producers of export products. One of the main announced purposes of these arrangements has been to eliminate any monopolistic exploitation by middlemen. Governments of developing countries have also actively intervened in the wage-determination process in their export sectors. In some cases this has taken mainly the form of creating conditions favorable for the establishment of effective trade unions and in others of setting minimum wages and of making wage awards. Workers in the export sector are now usually among the highest paid workers in the entire economy.

IV. THE NEW IMPERIALISM

The international aspects of capitalist development have received special attention from the followers of Marx. His ideas concerning colonial exploitation were expanded by Lenin into a theory of imperialism. Imperialism, according to Lenin, is the monopoly stage of capitalism in which free competition among many small firms is replaced to a large extent by monopolistic arrangements among large firms organized into international cartels and trusts. The territories of the world are divided among the great capitalist powers, as are the world's markets by these international capitalist monopolies. At this stage the less developed countries are important to capitalistic countries not only as sources of raw materials and markets for manufacturers but also as investment outlets for surplus capital. The exploitation of these markets becomes so significant as a means of staving off the inevitable destruction of capitalism that the capitalistic countries engage in imperialistic wars whose main objective is to redivide the political and economic control of the less developed economies. Lenin further argues that in this struggle among the capitalist powers the people of the underdeveloped countries gain nothing but instead become victims of colonial oppression and financial strangulation. As he says, "Finance capital and trusts are increasing instead of diminishing the differences in the rate of development of the various parts of world economy."[1]

Within the last few years there has been a considerable revival of interest in imperialism, particularly as it applies to the policies of the United States and other large industrial countries, as well as of the large international corporations, towards the developing countries. The so-called new imperialism differs from that which was described by Lenin mainly in form rather than substance. Proponents of the new imperialism argue, for example, that, although outright acquisition of colonies is largely a thing of the past, the major capitalist powers still attempt to control the less developed countries as a means of sustaining capitalism. Moreover, the objectives of this control are still the same as set forth by Marx and Lenin, that is: insuring an adequate supply of raw materials, providing markets for exports

[1] V. I. Lenin, *Imperialism, The Highest Stage of Capitalism,* New York: International Publishers, 1939, p. 96.

of manufactures, and establishing profitable outlets for the investment of capital.

It is alleged that foreign aid is one of the most important new techniques of control. The purpose of foreign aid such as provided by the United States to the developing countries is (so it is argued) to induce a favorable economic and political environment for foreign capital and imports. This objective is further promoted by military aid to friendly governments, by the maintenance of a network of military bases around the world as well as a globe-straddling navy, and—as in the past —by direct military interventions. The giant international corporations also are able to exercise considerable control over governments in less developed countries and thus protect and expand their supply sources and market outlets in these countries. In such countries as the United States there is, according to the critics of the supposed new imperialism, a basic unity of imperialist purpose in the foreign economic activities of industry and finance, in the overseas actions of the military, and in the activities of the diplomatic and foreign-aid services. The net effect of these alliances on the developing countries is to maintain their economic dependence on the major capitalistic powers.

The trouble with the theory of imperialism both in its old and new form is—as can be said about most sweeping yet simple theories—that the facts used to support its conclusions are also consistent with other hypotheses designed to explain the relations between developed capitalistic countries and the developing economies. Moreover, when the full range of economic and political relations between these two groups of countries is taken into account, these other, more complex analyses seem to stand up better than a simple Marxist version of imperialism. There is no question but that countries such as the United States have used their military and economic assistance programs as means of furthering their foreign policy interests. A major objective of postwar aid programs has been to prevent the expansion of communist influence in the developing countries by strengthening economically and militarily the noncommunistic governments of these countries. Even though one might grant that this policy has long been outdated in terms of the dangers of a monolithic communist movement to the United States or that the policy was sometimes badly administered, it by no means follows that the policy's true purpose was to maintain the status of less developed countries as suppliers of raw materials and outlets for foreign investment. Such factors as the types of development programs promoted by foreign aid, the difficulties of obtaining aid funds from the Congress as well as the drastic drop in these funds in recent years, and the relative unimportance of trade and investment flows between the United States and the developing countries are not consistent with a theory that pictures the government and the business community as sinister and deliberate exploiters of the underdeveloped world for the purpose of preventing capitalism from floundering. A large dose of mysticism must replace rationalism to fit such factors neatly into the theory of imperialism.

A more sophisticated version of imperialism maintains that even though the powerful industrial countries and large international firms may not deliberately set out to exploit the developing countries, the consequences of many of their policies are in fact imperialistic. This line of thought in turn raises the question of whether countries like the United States can modify their policies towards the developing nations and eliminate any imperialistic effects or whether capitalistic countries inevitably pursue imperialistic policies no matter how "good" the intentions of their individual citizens. The latter view is held by those who accept the doctrine of imperialism. The question is basically whether one accepts or rejects the Marxist-Leninist interpretation of history and analysis of capitalist development.

5

Recent Contributions (II)

Recent development theory has not, of course, just been devoted to explaining why more rapid growth failed to occur in the less developed nations. It has also been concerned with investigating the basic factors that cause development and the intersector and intertemporal processes by which capital accumulation and growth take place. This last of the chapters surveying development theories first considers the important link between the agricultural and industrial sectors during the growth process. Specifically, it examines the possibility of using surplus agricultural labor as a means of financing industrial development. The next section then outlines a new development theory that stresses the significance of certain noneconomic factors in shaping the kind of entrepreneurial personality that has been so important in the past. This emphasis upon the quality of the labor force is continued in the following section where the comparatively new subject of investment in human resources is discussed in relation to economic development. The chapter concludes by considering what is probably the most ambitious development theory formulated in recent years, namely, Rostow's stages theory of growth.

I. DEVELOPMENT IN A DUALISTIC ECONOMY

A frequency encountered concept in development economics is "dualism." The term is used to contrast various economic and

social differences that exist between the backward and more
advanced sectors of developing countries. For example, in urban
sectors, in comparison to most rural areas, more modern production techniques tend to be employed; a higher share of production is exchanged for other goods and services through the use
of money; the rate of population growth is lower; and the population may be more highly motivated in an economic sense. The
dualism notion is also sometimes employed to differentiate between that part of agriculture in which production is organized
on a large-scale modern basis, is export-oriented, and is largely
controlled by foreigners and that part in which production is
carried out on a very small scale by nonmarket-oriented, subsistence producers. However, in addition to being used to de-
scribe the characteristics of developing economies, the concept
of dualism forms the basis of some of the most important recent
theories of the growth process. In these development models
sectoral differences—usually those between urban and rural
areas—condition not only the nature of structural changes in
the economy but also the overall course of growth.

One important dualistic model focuses upon the manner in
which industrial growth takes place in those countries where
the pressures of a large rural population on a comparatively
small amount of arable land are especially strong (for example,
in India). In the densely populated rural areas of such underdeveloped countries labor productivity is extremely low. The
labor available on the typical family farm may never be fully
utilized in terms of a standard eight-hour working day, or is
employed fully only for short periods when the crops are being
planted or harvested. During the rest of the year, family workers are engaged in agricultural activities for only a few hours
a day. They may work each day up to the point where the
marginal productivity of an extra hour is zero, but not beyond.
The rest of the time they remain idle. Wage payments do not,
however, follow the marginal-productivity principle under a
family-farm system. Instead, the total output of the farm is divided among its members according to some institutional arrangement, perhaps on the basis of the average productivity of
the family members.

To take an extreme case, suppose there is no part of the year when family workers are all fully employed for eight hours a day. This means that some workers could leave the farms and take industrial jobs without a drop in total agricultural output, *provided* that the agricultural workers who are left increase their working time. To make another extreme assumption, suppose that the remaining workers are willing to work longer without receiving any higher wage per day. In other words, assume they would just as soon work up to eight hours a day as work five hours and remain idle the other three hours.

If the conditions outlined above prevail, a country can undertake economic development in a sense by lifting itself by its bootstraps. Workers can be bid away from agriculture to fill industrial jobs by offering them the traditional wage or slightly more than they have been receiving in agriculture. Those who remain on the farms take up the slack and maintain total agricultural output. Moreover, they are willing to do this without being paid more. But there is now more available agricultural output on a per worker basis, since fewer are left to share in the same total output. Suppose the government levied on the farm a tax equal to the value of the extra output now available. To meet this tax the family would have to sell the extra output for cash in the market place. With this tax money the government could pay the workers it bid away from the farms to undertake industrial production. With these cash wages the new industrial workers would, in turn, purchase the agricultural surplus the rest of the family had to sell to meet the new taxes. In effect, the extra output produced by the remaining farm workers has been used to provide food for the workers who left. The economy has gained, since agricultural output is still the same, yet industrial output has increased by the contribution of the new workers.

The same result could be attained without government intervention. For example, the head of the family may keep the surplus himself. But, instead of consuming it he may save most of it by, for example, purchasing industrial securities. The investment funds made available to industry in this manner would serve the same purpose as the tax-financed investment activity of the government.

As long as surplus labor existed in agriculture this type of bootstrap industrial development could continue with wages remaining constant. This would mean that, as industrial output expands by using more workers and machines, the proportion of profits in total industrial income rises. Since a large proportion of these are saved, this enables industrial development to proceed at an even faster rate. Finally, when all the surplus labor is eliminated from agriculture, this easy accumulation process comes to an end.

At this stage of full employment in agriculture, the removal of workers to the industrial sector decreases agricultural output. It is then no longer possible to pay the new industrial workers their former agricultural earnings without affecting the earnings of the workers who remain. When surplus labor ceases to exist, the old institutional rules determining wages also tend to be replaced by a wage system based on the marginal-productivity principle. Since at this "commercialization point" the marginal productivity of a fully employed agricultural worker rises as workers are withdrawn from this sector, the wage rate in agriculture, and therefore industry, will rise as the industrial sector expands. This wage increase cuts into industrial profits and tends to halt the rise in the share of profits in total income. Investment then no longer tends to grow faster than total income.

It should be emphasized that to run even this far the system requires a number of rather extreme assumptions. The most important is the existence of surplus labor, not just in a seasonal sense, but over an entire production cycle. More empirical work is needed, but the evidence collected so far indicates that surplus labor in the sense that the marginal productivity of labor is zero over the entire year does not exist. Consequently, agricultural output will decline from the beginning as agricultural workers are transferred to industry. If, however, the decline in output due to the loss of these workers is very small, it may still be possible to extract from agriculture a large part of their wages without reducing the incomes of the remaining workers, since average productivity of the remaining workers rises. But, additional saving from other sources will be required to complete the transfer. The government must also obtain the resources needed to provide the industrial labor force with capital equipment to work with, furnish them with homes, schools, hospitals, and so on; transport them to urban areas, and perhaps pay them for the higher real costs of living in urban areas. Another important assumption relates to the behavior of the agricultural workers who remain in the rural sector. In the absence of stringent tax measures these workers are likely to consume any increase in per capita output resulting from the withdrawal of agricultural labor. Thus, the saving needed to get the process going may not be forthcoming.

When we consider all these factors, painless development via the bootstrap method begins to look more and more like a neat theoretical exercise than an important practical possibility. Nevertheless, the analysis upon which it is based is important in that it focuses upon the interdependence between agricultural and industrial development in any economy. In particular, it stresses the point that if industrial expansion is to take place, provision must be made to furnish foodstuffs to the additional industrial workers. In practice this means that additional investment in the agricultural sector is necessary to undertake successful development in the industrial sector.

Once development in the rural sector reaches the stage where wages are determined by the same marginal-productivity principle that governs industrial wages, a key factor shaping the nature of development in the typical dualistic model is whether the capital/labor ratio tends to be higher in the manufacturing or in the agricultural sector. If manufacturing production is capital-intensive compared to agricultural (as seems to be the case in developing countries) and if incomes are initially high enough to permit the rate of capital accumulation to exceed the growth of population, the development process will be characterized by a higher growth rate for manufactures than agricultural output as well as a relative shift of the population to urban areas. The decline in the return to capital caused by its increased supply lowers the price of the more capital-using products, that is, manufactures relative to agricultural goods, and thus leads to an increase in the demand and production of manufactures compared to agricultural output. This shift is reinforced by the tendency to consume a higher proportion of manufactured goods as income rises, even if relative prices remain the same. However, the differential growth rates between the two sectors tend to narrow over time.

II. NONECONOMIC FACTORS IN DEVELOPMENT

The importance of noneconomic factors has long been stressed by many development writers. Marx is one who goes far beyond the traditional boundaries of economics in analyzing the growth process. However, even though economic change involves such socio-political phenomena as the class struggle, the basic direction of causality in the Marxian system still proceeds from economic factors to cultural conditions. Max Weber is an example of a writer who would reverse this causality. He believes the Calvinist ethic, with its emphasis on work and thrift, is the crucial element accounting for the success of Western capitalistic development. Among others who have emphasized the significance of non-economic factors as determinants of economic growth are Parsons, Veblen, Spengler, and Toynbee.

One of the most interesting and ambitious lines of thought concerning the role of noneconomic factors in development focuses upon the emergence of the "creative" or "achieving" personality type. Those who possess this personality seem to initiate economic innovation and progress, that is, they are entrepreneurs. Everett Hagen, a highly respected development economist who has become convinced of the inadequacy of a narrow economic approach to development, has made perhaps the most outstanding contribution in recent years to this line of analysis.[1]

Hagen first describes the traditional peasant-based society in which there is no significant economic growth. This society is custom-bound, hierarchical, and unproductive. The dominant personality type both among peasants and the elite classes is the authoritarian personality. Authoritarian individuals are uncreative people who perceive the world as an arbitrary place rather than as an orderly environment that is amenable to analysis and responds to their initiative. They resolve their relationships with

---

[1] E. E. Hagen, *On the Theory of Social Change*, Homewood, Ill.: Dorsey Press, 1962.

their fellow men mainly on the basis of arbitrary rules, and they avoid anxiety due to unresolved situations by relying upon tradition and the judgment of authority.

The traditional society is highly stable and can be changed only by powerful disruptive forces. The change begins, according to Hagen, when some important group in the society suffers a withdrawal of status respect, a condition that occurs when it is no longer respected by other important groups in the society. Hagen does not develop an explanation as to why the withdrawal of status respect takes place, but instead regards it as an historical accident. An illustration of its occurrence is when one traditional elite group forcibly displaces another traditional group from its social position.

Individuals who have lost status respect become frustrated and angry, but are powerless to affect society's attitude toward them. They are, however, able to vent part of their irritation on their families. Children, whose values are in the formative stage, are especially affected by the changed behavior of their fathers, and they are faced with a value conflict. They want to admire the traditional values of their fathers, but they know that to succeed they must develop a regard for the values of the group that is now in control. Their solution to this conflict is, according to Hagen, to deny both sets of values. They become retreatists in the sense that they do not expect much satisfaction from their socioeconomic role, nor do they expect to be socially accepted.

But, as Hagen says, this attitude is not a dead end. As it continues in successive generations, retreatism creates a home environment that is conducive to the emergence of the creative personality. Mothers eventually react against the negative attitudes of their husbands and begin to encourage their sons to succeed in the world as it is. The sons in turn gradually acquire the drive to achieve and the perception that achievement is possible. In short, they develop into creative personalities. Since economic prowess leads to social power and prestige, many are attracted into the economic world.

Hagen illustrates his theory with six historical cases of transition to economic growth. The countries that he analyzes are England, Japan, Colombia, Indonesia, Burma, and one case involving the Sioux Indians. In each instance he claims that his theory is supported by the development facts in these areas.

One of the difficulties with the theory is its generality. When rapid development occurs, it always seems possible to trace the history of the main participating groups far enough back to find a cycle of authoritarianism, withdrawal of status respect, retreatism, and creativity. Yet, the cycle seems so vague in some cases that we may rightly wonder whether sublimation of status withdrawal is always a significant part of major development efforts. At the same time, there seem to be many historical instances where status has been withdrawn from a group and nothing very remarkable ever emerged. Most would agree, however, that Hagen is following a promising line of inquiry. As Schumpeter and others pointed out long ago, there are often unique personality types who spark the development process in a country. There is an urgent need to know much more about how and why these individuals develop within a society.

III. INVESTMENT IN HUMAN RESOURCES

In surveying past development theories, it soon becomes apparent that most economists regarded capital accumulation as the key requirement for growth. The importance of improvements in the efficiency of the labor force is invariably dutifully noted, but that is about all. Actually, leaving aside broad sociological analyses of development, it is only in discussions of entrepreneurship that qualitative characteristics of individuals participating in the development process received much more than passing treatment. And even this analysis tends to be framed in general, nonoperational terms.

Recent studies of United States growth over the last 75 years (as well as of several European countries since 1950) have, however, raised serious doubts about the importance of quantitative increases in the capital stock as an explanatory variable for growth. Specifically, only a comparatively small part of the fourfold increase in United States per capita income from its 1869–1879 annual average level to its 1944–1953 annual average level can be accounted for either by the increase in capital stock or by the increase in the labor force. Apparently, "the complex of little understood forces" comprising what one writer calls "productivity" was the major source of economic development in this country. Several factors have been put forth as the major source of income gains. Technological progress is probably the most obvious, but improvements in resource allocation, economies of scale, and education have also been suggested.

Interest in the subject of investment in human resources, particularly in the form of education, has become widespread within the past few years in large part as a result of these growth studies. Physical capital is usually defined to include structures, durable equipment, commodity stocks, and foreign claims. However, one can broaden the concept of capital by also treating expenditures for education, job training, and health as investment outlays. Where education or health expenditures raise future earnings of the recipients, they represent investment outlays in the same sense as outlays for capital equipment. Schooling is an investment in human capital in the form of acquiring greater earning abilities. As Schultz remarks:

Truly, it can be said, the productive capacity of labor is predominantly a *produced* means of production. We thus "make" ourselves and to this extent "human resources" are a consequence of investments among which schooling is of major importance.[2]

Studies of the significance of investment in schooling as a causal factor in the income growth of the United States show that over 20% of the growth between 1929 and 1957 was due to increased education. This is more than the contribution made by the growth of physical capital during the same period. Another important source of growth between these years was what one investigator calls "advance in knowledge." The share of growth that can be allocated to this factor is 20%. However, in postwar northwest Europe the contribution of education to the growth rate of national income was only 5% in contrast to 14% for physical capital. Advances in knowledge added 16%.

Some people immediately rebel at the notion of treating educa-

---

[2] T. W. Schultz, *The Economic Value of Education,* New York: Columbia University Press, 1963, p. 10.

tion as an investment. They emphasize that there is much more to education than increasing one's earning capacity. In particular they stress the consumption component of schooling. The consumption benefits of education can be moral values, refinements in tastes, standards of conduct, and other present or future sources of satisfaction. Should there be too much focus on the productivity-raising aspects of education, some fear that these fundamental but nonquantifiable benefits from education may be neglected.

It would be wrong to dismiss this point as a typical fear of the nonscientific. Unless conscious efforts are made to consider both the consumption and investment benefits of educational expenditures simultaneously, a long-run misallocation of these outlays in either direction can easily result. This, of course, does not mean that the investment aspects of schooling should be ignored.

The main question that arises in treating education as an investment is whether there is a proper balance between investment in material capital and investment in human capital. The rate of return to schooling can be measured in much the same way that the rate of return on a piece of capital equipment is determined. The costs of education should include not only the direct outlays for teacher salaries, equipment, and so on, but also the indirect costs of the foregone earnings by the students. If possible, some deduction should also be made from these total costs to take account of school costs that provide only consumption benefits. The returns from education are the increase in earnings that are associated with additional schooling. The rate of return to any schooling level can be computed by applying standard discounting procedures to the relevant cost and benefit figures. If the percentage rate of return on education is substantially higher than the percentage return earned on material capital in business, then there is underinvestment in schooling.

There are now a fair number of studies estimating rates of return on investment in education in developing countries. Most of these show that rates of return to educational investment either fall with more schooling or first rise and then fall. While there are considerable differences among the countries in the level of social rates of return, yields on primary education of between 15 and 20% and on college education of between 10 and 15% are typical in many of the studies. In the United States, the first 4 years of schooling yield a 100% return, the next 4 a return of 18%, and a college education between 8 and 9%. Much more study is needed in this field in order (1) to produce comprehensive and comparable estimates of rates of return in developing countries and (2) to relate differences in these rates to such factors as differences in the pattern of education attainment levels of the population. However, it is clear that expenditures on education—particularly for primary and secondary education—represent a highly worthwhile use of resources in developing countries even when judged on limited economic grounds.

IV. STAGES OF GROWTH

Of all the names associated with recent contributions to development theory, few are better known than W. W. Rostow. Such standard development terms as "the preconditions for take-off," "the take-off," and "self-sustained growth" were coined by him. There is hardly a political leader in the developing nations who is not familiar with these cliches, if not always with the content behind them. Rostow's major work, *The Stages of Economic Growth*,[3] actually carries the subtitle, *A Non-Communist Manifesto*, and was presented to political leaders and scholars in the developing and developed nations as an alternate theory to the self-defeating pattern of capitalist growth outlined by Marx. Like the Marxian analysis, however, Rostow's model of the growth process has been considerably more influential on a political and popular level than among professional economists and historians.

A. Rostow's Five Stages

According to Rostow, there are five stages of economic growth: the traditional society, the preconditions for take-off, the take-off, the drive to maturity, and the age of high mass consumption. His description of the traditional society is rather similar to Hagen's or, for that matter, to the low-level equilibrium economy dis-

---

[3] W. W. Rostow, *The Stages of Economic Growth: A Non-Communist Manifesto*, Cambridge: University Press, 1960.

cussed in the preceding chapter. The social structure is hierarchical, and the value system is geared to long-run fatalism. But the essence of the traditional society is that it possesses a low ceiling of attainable output per head because of the backward nature of its technology. As Rostow says, its production capabilities are based on pre-Newtonian science and technology and pre-Newtonian attitudes towards the physical world.

The second stage of growth, during which the preconditions for take-off are developed, involves important noneconomic and economic changes. In the noneconomic sphere what is significant is the emergence of a new elite who regard economic modernization as being not only possible but also highly desirable. From this group comes those who are willing to mobilize savings and undertake innovational risks. However, more than sociological and psychological changes take place at this stage. Usually a rise of nationalism in reaction against intrusion from more advanced nations is also a powerful motive force. Rostow cites Commodore Perry's visit to Japan in the 1850's as an event leading to reactive nationalism and economic modernization.

In the economic area the preconditions stage involves such fundamental changes as a rise in the rate of capital accumulation above the rate of population growth, the exploitation of existing innovational opportunities as well as the creation of new ones, and the training of labor for specialized, large-scale production. For example, increased investment and innovational activity occurs in the agricultural sector and creates a surplus that can be used to finance industrial expansion. Similarly, substantial investment in transportation facilities and other forms of social overhead capital is undertaken during this period.

The third period, the take-off, is the crucial one. It is at this stage that the resistance to steady growth is finally overcome and growth becomes a normal condition. In the preconditions stage significant economic progress takes place, but the society is still characterized by traditional attitudes and productive techniques. But in the take-off period, the growth process becomes institutionalized in the society.

The take-off is defined more precisely by Rostow as involving all of the following changes. First, the rate of net investment rises from 5% or less to over 10% of national income. Second, one or

more new, substantial, and rapidly growing manufacturing industries arise. Third, a political, social, and institutional framework emerges that is highly favorable to sustained growth. On
the basis of the historical experience of such countries as Great
Britain, Japan, the United States, and Russia, Rostow concludes
that the take-off period lasts only about 20 years. Thereafter
comes a period of some 40 years that he terms "the drive to
maturity." During this period modern technology spreads beyond
the leading sectors that powered the take-off to all major parts
of the economy. To use Rostow's words, in this stage "an economy
demonstrates that it has the technological and entrepreneurial
skill to produce not everything, but anything it chooses to
produce."[4]

Thereafter, the economy moves into "the age of high mass-
consumption" when the leading sectors shift towards the production of durable consumers' goods and services. At this stage incomes have risen to levels where basic food, shelter, and clothing
no longer are the main consumption objectives of the labor force.
Automobiles, TV sets, refrigerators, and so on, are now the items
that catch the interest of consumers. In addition, the economy,
through its political process, expresses a willingness to allocate
increased resources to social welfare and security. Rostow cites
the United States, most of the nations of Western Europe, and
Japan as countries which have reached this stage, and he thinks
that even the Soviet Union is ready for it.

B. Conclusions

Rostow's stages-analysis is the most recent of a long list of development approaches based on this concept. Marx himself viewed
history as a cycle of revolution, progressive evolution, the rise of
resistance to institutional change, degeneration, and again revolution. He thought he could discern four social systems that had
already gone through this cycle or were in the process of going
through these steps: namely, primitive communism, the ancient
slave state, feudalism, and capitalism. The German historical
school was also very strong on the concept of stages. We find

---

[4] Ibid., p. 10.

authors in this tradition viewing development as occurring in such stages as the household economy, the town economy, and the national economy; barter, the money economy, and the credit economy; and savagery, the pastoral life, agriculture, and manufactures; and finally agriculture, manufacturing, and trade.

It is easy to find historical experience that seems to verify these various sequences. But, as the multiplicity of stage theories suggests, there does not appear to be any one stage sequence that applies in any meaningful way to a broad sweep of development experience. Of course, it is not hard to see that there are significant development differences between countries such as India and the United States. But the essence of a stages theory is that development must proceed in a particular sequence of clearly definable steps. Moreover, the analytical relationships of any particular stage to the preceding and subsequent stage must be specified in sufficient detail that all can agree upon when these connections have been completed.

Most economists think that Rostow has failed to meet these requirements for a valid stages theory. They regard his concept more as an impressionistic interpretation of a wide sweep of historical experience than as a rigorous, scientific analysis. Take, for example, Rostow's distinction between the preconditions period and the take-off. Most economic historians fail to see the sharp distinction between these periods that he apparently does. In the preconditions stage Rostow stresses the transformation of agriculture and the extensive investment in social overhead capital. Then, in the take-off period he points to "a particular sharp stimulus," such as a major industrial innovation that sets in motion a chain of secondary expansion. But do not these various activities take place more or less simultaneously, or at least in a nondiscontinuous manner? Agricultural development and increases in social overhead capital in and of themselves initiate modern economic growth just as industrial expansion stimulates further growth in agriculture and in the economy's infrastructure. To attempt to separate these activities seems highly arbitrary, especially since statistical evidence does not support his contention about the doubling of the investment ratio in the take-off period. Not only is the division arbitrary, but it can be highly misleading, if development policies are formulated on the basis of this dichotomy. From Rostow's theory we get the impression that a country should turn to vigorous industrial development efforts only after agriculture has been modernized and the stock of social overhead capital greatly increased. Yet, postwar growth experience in the developing countries has convinced more and more development economists that the agricultural and industrial sectors must expand side by side if growth is to be more than the establishment of a few flashy industries or the creation of an agricultural surplus that soon disappears into a larger rural population.

6

Programs and Policies

Although economists have learned a great deal about the processes of economic growth during the last 20 years, we are still a long way from a generally accepted development theory. We are at an early stage of undertaking the kind of detailed country-by-country studies and general statistical investigations necessary to test many unsubstantial hypotheses about the development process.

Yet, political leaders in the developing nations cannot wait until the economics profession agrees on a single theory of economic development. These leaders are committed to raising the rate of per capita income growth here and now and they must make specific policy decisions for the best way of achieving this goal. Should they try to increase investment activity over the whole range of production, or should they concentrate on a few industries or sectors? Should they stress education instead of building roads? What levels of formal schooling should be emphasized? Is it wise to increase the government's investment program with deficit financing?

These are but a few of the issues that face the developing nations. The purpose of the next three chapters is to point out what the main policy problems are and to summarize the major areas of agreement and disagreement. We do not have final answers by any means. Nevertheless, the development analyses outlined in the previous chapters do provide the basis for reducing the areas of controversy in development planning.

I. THE "BIG-PUSH" VERSUS
THE SELECTIVE APPROACH

The most fundamental policy issue that policymakers must decide is whether to attempt a massive, big-push development effort or to concentrate upon raising growth rates in selective, key sectors. Many economists maintain that successful development requires a large-scale investment program involving many different lines of production. One of them says:

There is a minimum level of resources that must be devoted to . . . a development program if it is to have any chance of success. . . . Proceeding "bit-by-bit" will not add up in its effects to the sum total of the single bits. A minimum quantum of investment is a necessary condition of success.[1]

Other economists believe that a more modest, selective growth effort is the only feasible program to follow. The doctrine of large-scale, balanced growth is, in the view of one writer in this group, "an incomplete, implausible, and even potentially dangerous solution"[2] to breaking out of the low income levels of underdevelopment.

Proponents of the "all-out" approach base their case on the profit interdependencies that exist among different investment projects. The indivisibility of capital inputs leads to production conditions in which unit costs, instead of being constant at all output levels, decrease significantly as output expands until the scale of production becomes large. Cost curves in industries that make up the social overhead capital of the economy, such as power, communications, and transportation, behave in this fashion. But, so also do cost curves in many manufacturing industries. Markets in underdeveloped countries for some of these products are so small that unit costs are above effective demand at all output

---

[1] P. N. Rosenstein-Rodan, "Notes on the Theory of the 'Big Push,'" in H. S. Ellis, ed., *Economic Development for Latin America,* London: Macmillan and Co., 1962, p. 57.
[2] H. W. Singer, *International Development: Growth and Change,* New York: McGraw-Hill Book Co., 1964, p. 50.

levels. Consequently, these items are not produced domestically. According to the "big-push" proponents, it is necessary to bring about a large increase in demand in order to establish these important industries—to say nothing of bringing unit costs down to minimum levels.

In discussing profit interdependence among investment projects, the "big-push" advocates are utilizing the concept of external economies that was mentioned in Chapter 2. In particular they stress the importance of externalities that work on the demand side. Rosenstein-Rodan's classic illustration of the shoe industry best brings out their point.

If a hundred workers who were previously in disguised unemployment (so that the marginal productivity of their labour was equal to zero) in an underdeveloped country are put into a shoe factory, their wages will constitute additional income. If the newly employed workers spend all of their additional income on the shoes they produce, the shoe factory will find a market and will succeed. In fact, however, they will not spend all of their additional income on shoes. There is no easy solution of creating an additional market in this way. The risk of not finding a market reduces the incentive to invest, and the shoe factory investment project will probably be abandoned. Let us vary the example. Instead of putting a hundred previously unemployed workers in one shoe factory, let us put ten thousand workers in one hundred factories and farms which between them will produce the bulk of the wage-goods on which the newly employed workers will spend their wages. What is not true in the case of one single shoe factory will become true for the complementary system of one hundred factories and farms. The new producers will be each other's customers and will verify Say's Law by creating an additional market. The complementarity of demand will reduce the risk of not finding a market. Reducing such interdependent risks naturally increases the incentive to invest.[3]

The case for the "big-push" thus rests on two points. First, the existence of significant economies of scale in many productive lines means that the demand for many items must be high even for a break-even point to exist. It must be even higher to achieve the lowest production costs possible. Second, to raise the demand for any one particular line it is usually necessary to raise income

[3] P. N. Rosenstein-Rodan, *op. cit.*, p. 62.

levels appreciably over the entire economy. This, in turn, can only be accomplished with a massive, all-out investment program.

The critics of this approach grant that the argument is valid as far as it goes. But, they claim, it rests on special supply assumptions that are unlikely to be fulfilled in less developed countries. Rosenstein-Rodan, for example, assumes in the foregoing quotation that all ten thousand workers put into the hundred factories and farms were previously unemployed in a disguised sense. The same must be true for the workers who are involved in producing specialized capital goods and material inputs used by these factories and farms. Therefore, the output of the new industries is obtained without decreasing output in other sectors nor bidding up wage rates. The supply of capital must also be highly elastic, either from domestic or foreign sources, in order to prevent interest rates from rising and dampening the profitability prospects of investment.

If the supplies of labor, capital, and natural resources are not perfectly elastic, then factor prices and cost curves rise at the same time as efforts to increase demand are being undertaken. Should factor supplies be completely inelastic, a "big-push" effort will raise costs more than demand and increase the unprofitability of expansion by particular firms. Actually, the supply situation in most developing countries is, of course, neither completely inelastic nor completely elastic. In the recent past many development economists thought that disguised unemployment was widespread in the heavily populated, developing countries. Consequently, they thought that the bootstrap method of growth described in Chapter 4, especially if supplemented with heavy foreign aid, offered a quick and easy answer to the development problem. More experience and careful empirical investigations have shattered most of these optimistic expectations. As mentioned in Chapter 4, disguised unemployment in the sense of zero marginal productivity over the entire year does not appear to be widespread in heavily populated rural areas, if it exists at all. Moreover, it is now perfectly clear that there are crucial shortages of entrepreneurs, managers, technicians, and skilled workers of all sorts, and that any massive investment program puts a tremendous strain on these resources. The more common view now is that resource inelasticity is an effective barrier in most less developed countries to a successful "big-push" investment effort.

This does not mean that the situation is hopeless. It implies that economists and policymakers alike must abandon this escapist, unreal solution and grapple with the hard realities of growth. There are particular industries and sectors in which intensive investment efforts can pay high dividends by eliminating bottlenecks and stimulating a higher investment rate in other industries. In these leading sectors investment complementarities and resource elasticity can be effectively utilized.

Pointing to the potentialities of a more selective approach to growth does not mean that we can simply forget about balance in the development process. Obviously we cannot ignore either the technical input-output relations of production or the demand patterns of consumers. As more people are brought into industry, domestic agricultural output must be expanded or farm imports increased if this industrial growth is not to be choked by raising food prices. Likewise, if farm incomes are to rise steadily, the greater demand for manufactures on the part of farmers must somehow be met and, on a more detailed commodity level, there are thousands of similar interrelationships. Any successful development program must proceed on enough fronts to meet the balances that these interrelations involve. But this still leaves a wide range of choice concerning the best activities to undertake and the degree to push different output lines.

In the "all-out" approach every industry takes a giant step forward. This includes consumption-goods industries in the manufacturing and agricultural sectors, capital-goods industries, and even social-overhead investments. Under the selective approach, giant steps are taken only in a relatively small number of productive lines at any one time. For example, large investments might be made in such projects as a multipurpose dam, an oil refinery, a steel mill, a road between two important cities, or an irrigation scheme. At the same time, public authorities must be sure that small investment steps are being taken throughout the rest of the economy's productive structure. Without this, the economy will be unable to secure, either by direct production or trade, the greater amounts of many other goods and services that consumers desire when their per capita income levels rise. In short, selectivity must still involve overall balance. Giant steps on all lines are physically impossible; giant steps in a small number of lines are physically possible but are soon likely to lead to economic imbalances. Steady across-the-board progress coupled with big steps in selective sectors seems to be the best policy.

II. THE ROLE OF THE GOVERNMENT

The conclusion that a selective approach to investment activity is the best policy for the developing countries to follow makes the problem of just how to proceed even more difficult. The "all-out" approach is to undertake heavy investment everywhere. Under the selective approach, it is necessary to pick and choose carefully among investment alternatives. How does a developing country decide which of the various alternatives are the most productive, both directly and for stimulating further growth? How does the country avoid causing interindustry and inter-sector imbalances that can thwart successful development?

The private sector might handle these matters through the price system. Private investors in pursuit of profits could seek out the most productive investment activities. Not many people would go along with this position, however. A case for government intervention in the market mechanism can be made even under the standard of complete consumer sovereignty because of certain conditions that can prevent even a free market mechanism from allocating resources in an efficient manner. The main ones on the production side are: (1) the existence of indivisible or lumpy capital units; (2) the existence of collective or public goods; (3) the existence of technological externalities; and (4) the existence of imperfect markets.

As mentioned in the preceding section, the indivisibility of capital results in decreasing unit costs over a wide output range. If the market for a product subject to this condition is only large enough to support a few firms of optimum size, monopolistic pricing and output policies, which are socially inefficient, will emerge. Collective or public goods are commodities that are consumed collectively by members of the community. The protective services given to a community by a flood-control project illustrates this point. The essential aspect of these commodities is that they are not—usually for institutional reasons—subject to the exclusion principle. When one individual consumes the service, other individuals also consume it, that is, your flood-control protection can be my flood-control protection. A free-market pricing system will generally result in the underproduction of these goods from a social point of view. One reason is that each consumer, in an attempt to induce others to pay for the collective good, tends to understate his true preferences for the product.

Technological spillover effects arise because of physical interdependence among different productive lines. A change in the input or output rate by one producer affects the physical output other producers can obtain from their physical inputs. An example is the damage caused to others when some firms pollute rivers and streams with waste products. Since individual producers do not take into account the effect of such actions on others, a socially optimum allocation of resources will not be achieved. The fourth impediment to the achievement of allocative efficiency under a free-price system is the existence of imperfect markets. An important example of such an imperfection is a lack of knowledge concerning the profit interdependencies among different investment projects. Other market causes of inefficiency are resource rigidities, irrational behavior, and monopolistic practices.

All four of these conditions cause inefficient resource allocation from the consumers' point of view. Consequently, some form of government intervention is justifiable. It can range from regulatory actions to direct investment and production activity. This depends on the specific nature of the misallocation and the relative efficiency of government versus private production. Specific industries in which intervention is likely to be needed for greater efficiency are electric power, communications, education, and defense.

Most governments of developing nations go considerably further than this in their market intervention because they are unwilling to be guided entirely by individual preferences. The best example of this rejection of free-market forces is in the saving and investment area. Many political leaders believe that the present generation does not give sufficient weight in its saving decisions to the needs of future generations. Contemporary households are too shortsighted and devote too large a share of their incomes to consumption purposes. These political leaders believe it is the duty of the government to represent future as well as present generations and consequently they take measures to increase the rate of present saving and investment.

A desire to change the distribution of income from what it would be under a completely free-price system is another important reason for government intervention. This applies not only to the present income distribution but also over the long haul. Governments also sometimes do not wish to accept consumer preferences with respect to particular goods. Many governments try to redirect spending away from luxury consumption goods toward "essential" consumer products or even investment goods. Finally, governments seek all sorts of noneconomic goals, such as maintaining political stability and creating certain social attitudes. The fact that these goals can be influenced by investment policies is another reason why governments are unwilling to leave the allocation process entirely to the free-market mechanism.

III. DEVELOPMENT PLANNING

There are almost as many forms of government intervention in the investment process as there are reasons given for such intervention. Governments can raise investment funds by taxation and then make the funds available on a competitive basis to private investors. Tax and subsidy policies can be used to curtail or encourage the output of any particular commodity. Or governments themselves can undertake investment activities and also employ elaborate quantitative controls to help direct resources into the productive lines they wish to see expanded. There is, of course, considerable variation among less developed countries in the form of intervention, but direct participation in the investment process is now fairly extensive. In Brazil and India, for example, 45% and 60%, respectively, of total investment is undertaken by each government.

Because of the importance of both direct and indirect intervention, it has become almost essential for governments to engage in development planning. The term "planning" means merely "that the government has organized its decision-making processes so as to take account of all the economic effects of each of its acts, the total program of actions being a coherent one designed to achieve as rapid an economic growth as is consistent with other national goals."[4] By means of these planning efforts, the developing countries attempt to determine the best set of investment alternatives to adopt. There are wide differences, however, in the level of planning activity among these countries. They range from a government simply dressing up its traditional capital budget and calling it a development plan, to detailed plans for all major industries, as in Yugoslavia. The description that follows will present the major steps, which fall between these two extreme positions, in development planning undertaken by such nations as India.

The first step is to determine a tentative growth target for the economy over the planning period (usually five years). At first this may be set by merely extrapolating the past growth trend of national product and modifying this result on the basis of general knowledge concerning prospective economic changes. A more formal method is to estimate the ratio of saving (from both domestic and foreign sources) to national product under expected policy conditions and then to divide this ratio by an estimate of the incremented capitol-output ratio during the planning period. For example, as explained in Chapter 3, if the saving-income ratio is 10% and the incremental capital-output ratio is 3, then the annual growth rate will be 3.3%. The problem with this method is to come up with an accurate estimate of the capital-output ratio. The difficulties of making such estimates were emphasized in Chapter 3 along with the limitations of this whole approach as a forecasting method. Nevertheless, it still is useful as a rough guide to the feasibility of various aggregate development rates. If growth rates for per capita income are desired, a population estimate is, of course, also needed.

Given an initial growth target for gross national product over the planning period, the next step is to break this figure down into government expenditures, private consumption, gross investment, and exports. These four uses of resources must be equal

---

[4] Everett E. Hagen, *Planning Economic Development,* Homewood: Richard D. Irwin, 1963, p. 1.

to the total resources available to the economy, that is, gross domestic product plus imports.

When the planners have agreed upon a division of the national product into these broad components, they then consider the main industrial sectors in the economy, such as agriculture, transportation and communications, manufacturing, trade and services, and housing. Their objective is to project not only output levels in these sectors, but also the investment required to achieve these levels and the uses of the outputs for consumption, investment, and other purposes. Although most countries that plan on a sector basis actually use rough projection methods based on historical trends for determining the many different magnitudes needed, a sophisticated technique is first to estimate final demands for the products of these sectors by using income-elasticities information on them. Next the outputs needed in various sectors to support these final demands are determined by using an input-output model of the economy. If such a model is available, it is possible to handle the problem of making the inputs and outputs of the various sectors consistent with each other. Otherwise, rough balancing techniques must be employed to make sure, for example, that steel output is just sufficient to meet the final direct demand for steel and the indirect demand for it as an input component in many other final products.

The output estimates of the various sectors are not determined just by private demand-and-supply conditions. As mentioned earlier, most governments wish to modify the composition of total output that would occur under free markets. The government may want a steel mill or an irrigation project in a particular geographic region for noneconomic reasons. At this stage, these projects must be introduced into the multisector analysis. It is also necessary to estimate the manpower requirements of the various sectors and check these against the availability of different types of labor. If labor coefficients have been computed for various industries, a rough approximation of manpower needs can be made by multiplying the projected outputs of these industries by their appropriate labor coefficients and then breaking the aggregate labor required for each industry into the various skill categories of the industry. Estimates of the possibilities of satisfying these requirements can be made by surveying current manpower supplies and by computing the flows of newly trained workers from schools and on-the-job training programs. Should manpower needs and availabilities differ widely, it is necessary to modify the plan to establish this consistency condition.

The last step in formulating a development plan is to select the particular set of investment projects and production techniques in all sectors that enable the country to achieve its growth in the most economically efficient manner. In many ways this part of the development process is the most crucial. This is the stage in which investment funds are committed to specific projects, and the choices made are crucial to the success or failure of the development program. Up to this point, only a very broad and tentative allocation of investment funds, based on historical relationships, is made. Now the most socially productive uses of the investment funds are determined.

In many sectors it may be decided that private investors who are guided by the profit motive can best handle the investment problem. In others, where there are reasons to believe that there is a significant divergence between social and private productivity, the government may direct the investment process. Just as private investors select those projects where the *private* marginal productivity of capital is the highest, the government should pick those investments which have the highest *social* marginal productivity. In doing this, government decision makers must modify the revenue and cost calculations private investors make insofar as these figures do not reflect actual social benefits and social costs. For example, if the marginal productivity of labor in agriculture were zero, the social cost of using some of this labor in other activities would be zero, since no agricultural output would be lost in the shift. In calculating the net social benefits derived from using the labor in these other endeavors, the wages paid to this labor should not be deducted from total benefits.[5] Similarly, the favorable effects of technological externalities, as well as any unfavorable distortions, should be brought into the calculations of net benefits. In practice, a lack

---

[5] If, however, the labor must be transported to a new area and provided with new housing and public services, these costs must be deducted from total benefits.

of adequate data regarding many of these factors means that it is worthwhile to calculate only the most obvious causes of divergence between social and private productivity. Government planners must also be careful to stop their investment activities prior to the point where the social productivity of government investment becomes less than the social productivity of private investment efforts.

Once calculations of social profitability have been made for a series of interrelated investment projects, it is necessary to begin working backward and modifying the nature of the plan. The investment prospects for particular products may be so dismal that it is cheaper to import them rather than follow the tentative plan of expanding domestic production. Or it may be that some combination of an increase in imports and domestic products is the best policy to follow. The determination of the most efficient method of producing any output increase in terms of the type and quality of raw materials, labor, and capital equipment obviously can result in quite different output and labor requirements than had been previously planned for. It is even appropriate to change the total volume of investment by borrowing more from international lending institutions, if the rate of return on marginal projects under the initial investment allocation is above the international borrowing rate. In short, planners must keep revising as more information becomes available until a consistent plan that is economically efficient within certain political constraints is formulated.

In view of important changes that can result from detailed calculations of the social productivity of alternative investment projects, the question often arises as to why the whole planning process does not start at this detailed stage rather than at an aggregative level. Many countries do in fact start with the submission of lists of specific investment projects. When the economy is quite simple and the government's role is small, this is the best procedure to follow. The construction of elaborate planning models in these conditions is itself a socially unproductive investment activity. But, when a government attempts to alter significantly the pattern of growth that would occur under the private-market mechanism in terms of both the proportion of investment to gross domestic product and of the composition of output, this is not the best procedure. Planners need the guidelines established under the first two steps in the planning process in order to begin to select appropriate investment projects. Otherwise, they would undertake all sorts of needless calculations as well as miss many that are needed.

Development planning as actually practiced by the noncentrally planned, developing nations must generally be considered a failure. In some cases the plans set forth by governments have been rightly regarded as unrealistic political propaganda. They have soon been completely ignored, even by the officials who made them. In many other instances, the failure of planning has been due to the poor performance by planners in predicting output levels on an industry-by-industry basis and even in terms of broad economic sectors. Frequently by the time a plan has been published, the existing state of economic affairs has proved to be very different from the initial conditions on which the plan depended.

The act of adopting a development plan in a centrally planned economy is quickly followed by a series of commands to enterprises to produce specific output levels. When such economies are well endowed with trained personnel and can effectively hold down consumption levels, they usually are able to carry out their development goals with reasonable success. In mixed economies of the developing nations, on the other hand, adopting a plan results at best in the issuance of specific production orders only to the government sector. Even in this sector, planners often do not have the authority or personnel to ensure that a serious effort is made to achieve the specified goals. As far as output in the private sector is concerned, the government can only use indirect means, such as taxes and subsidies, to obtain the production goals set forth in the plan. The likelihood of badly estimating responses in this sector is very high. Moreover, when production in key private sectors is very different from that which was planned, output performance in the government sector is also likely to differ widely from its planned levels because of the dependence of any one industry's output on the outputs of other industries.

Despite the failure of most planning in the less developed economies, development specialists generally believe that it can be highly useful. Sound planning can reveal the bottlenecks likely to retard potential growth, and in most economies there are politically and economically feasible means of easing some of these bottlenecks. However, if growth goals are set unrealistically high, the entire planning exercise becomes meaningless in these terms.

7

Development Policies In Major Economic Sectors

Because of the many differences in economic conditions among less developed countries, there is no one particular pattern of development that produces the fastest growth rate for all developing nations. The specific set of industries that is optimal for any country must be determined on the basis of the investment criteria just outlined. Nevertheless, on the basis of the theoretical analysis already presented and of the postwar-development experience, some useful generalizations concerning development policy can be made with respect to broad economic sectors.

I. THE AGRICULTURAL SECTOR

Often the most crucial sector is agriculture. As pointed out in Chapter 1, this is the sector in which most of the people in developing countries live and in which productivity per person is the lowest in the economy. The key question is how to raise the productivity level in the agricultural sector. Not only is such an increase needed simply to raise living standards but it is also necessary to provide the agricultural surplus required to finance increased manufacturing activity. However, until comparatively recent years most developing countries tended to sacrifice agricultural development to industrialization efforts. It took the near-famine conditions in South Asia during the mid-sixties to shift development priorities significantly towards the agricultural sector in many countries.

There seems to be no single, simple way to solve the agricultural problem. An important lesson learned in the postwar period is that land reform, improvements in transportation and marketing facilities, the establishment of better credit facilities, and more productive agricultural techniques are all needed to meet the problem successfully.

One aspect of agricultural behavior that is being increasingly appreciated and utilized in planning activities is the generally high degree of responsiveness on the part of farmers to economic incentives. For a long time many authorities in developing countries, particularly colonial authorities, did not believe this to be true. They viewed peasant producers and farm laborers as individuals who wanted only to reach a relatively low target income. Once this income level was reached, it was felt that any increase in prices or wages simply reduced market supplies, since farmers could achieve their target income by offering less on the market. Authorities who thought this was the typical agricultural behavior pattern usually adopted one of three approaches. They threw up their hands and said nothing would work; they tried to extract what surplus was available by taxation; or they tried by all sorts of rules and regulations to force the farmers to adopt better techniques. The first approach can be followed under colonial rule, but not, of course, under nationalist leadership. The trouble with the second pattern is that the government generally is not able to force out enough surplus to carry out its industrialization plans. The last method is likely to result merely in further frustrations that confirm the old views about the nonresponsiveness of farmers.

Yet, there is now an abundance of evidence from Africa, Southeast Asia, and Latin America contradicting this belief. This does not mean that a country merely has to juggle a few prices to achieve agricultural development. That would be ridiculous. It means that developing countries can build their programs on the premise that farmers will respond to appropriate incentives. Otherwise it would be necessary to undertake costly and time-consuming efforts to change basic values and attitudes before effective measures could be taken.

A basic task in agriculture is to develop market opportunities for existing producers. Sometimes there are good markets for products, but such cost factors as monopolistic interest rates, inadequate transportation and storage facilities, and high costs of fertilizers prevent producers from taking advantage of them. In many instances government-investment activities in these areas yield high social returns in opening up these markets. Creating a stable market is especially important for inducing subsistence producers to switch to cash crops. These producers remember only too well instances in which they shifted entirely to a cash crop when its price was high only to face a market collapse a year or so later or to find that the new crop was wiped out by some disease. They reason that at least they will not starve if they stick with their traditional subsistence crop. To overcome this understandable attitude, it is usually appropriate to establish marketing boards which stabilize producer prices. These should not, however, degenerate into schemes for taxing away most of the farmers' agricultural surplus. Other ways of helping to overcome the difficulties of establishing cash agriculture are to provide liberal credit facilities for carrying farmers over more than a single season and to undertake research to discover disease-resistant seeds.

The development of high-yielding varieties of grains—the so-called Green Revolution—has dramatically increased the willingness of subsistence producers to adopt new, more productive methods of farming. The 20–40% increase in yields that could be achieved from the use of fertilizers with old varieties was not sufficient to overcome the kinds of risks outlined above. However, the 300–400% yield increase associated with the new varieties has been sufficient to overcome these risks. In Asia, for example, the total area planted to new seeds rose from about 5 million acres in 1966–1967 to 34 million in 1968–1969.

The agricultural revolution, however, has not spread as yet to Latin America, outside of Mexico. A major barrier to achieving high levels of productivity in much of Latin America seems to be the system of land tenure. Many laborers and sharecroppers in these countries do not possess the incentive to raise productivity that they would have if they owned their own land. The owners of these large estates also are not particularly interested in raising productivity. It should be emphasized that land reform will not solve all problems. First, care must be taken not to break up agricultural holding to below the most efficient size farm. Next, it must be remembered that new small landowners will need even more of the kind of help that was discussed above in connection with subsistence farmers. Most economists agree, however, that there is considerable room for land reforms in developing countries.

In those parts of the world where the Green Revolution has already been successful, attention has been shifted to the consideration of the so-called second-generation problems related to the agricultural breakthrough. These are the problems that must be solved if the income-raising impact of the new varieties and techniques is to be sustained and widened. One such problem is the danger that the new varieties may be attacked by diseases to which they are not resistant. The example of Ireland's potato famine in the late 1840's shows that this possibility should be considered very seriously. The blight that affected potatoes caused the death of a million and a half Irishmen. Continued research and testing to minimize such a possibility with the new grain varieties is essential.

Another important "second generation problem" is to provide expanding markets for the increasing agricultural surplus. Just as Rosenstein-Rodan's shoe workers are not going to spend all of their increased incomes on shoes, agricultural producers cannot lift a country's income level very far by selling additional output to each other. A market outside of the rural sector is also needed.

If the economy is a closed one, the only source of demand is the industrial sector, which must be growing to provide an outlet for increased agricultural production. But, since developing economies engage in international trade, the additional agricultural output can be used to replace existing imports of foodstuffs or can be exported to other countries. International trade frees a country from the constraints of balanced growth.

The developed countries could be a major market outlet for the increased agricultural production of the developing nations.

Unfortunately, too many of these markets are reserved for local producers. For example, Japan supports the internal price of rice at a level three times that in the world market. The encouragement given to Japanese production from this policy has not only forced the government to cut off all imports but has even resulted in a surplus that is dumped on the world rice market. The policy of high price supports for agricultural products followed by the European Community has also resulted in a sharp reduction in imports of wheat and feed grains into this important market. One of the most important contributions that these and most other developed countries can make to the welfare of the developing nations (and to their own welfare as well) is to begin to dismantle the highly inefficient and costly systems of agricultural protection that have been allowed to build up in these countries.

II. MANUFACTURING ACTIVITY

Developing countries were traditionally told that the best way to build up the manufacturing sector was to follow the indirect approach of specializing initially upon primary-product exports and thereby induce the development of some local industry as income and demand levels rose. Needless to say, this is advice that few countries are willing to accept these days without substantial modification. Most political and economic leaders in the developing countries regard industrialization as the key to solving their goals of higher per capita incomes and greater employment opportunities. They consider both the extent and rate of industrialization induced by specializing on primary-product exports to be insufficient. Moreover, many think that colonial rulers deliberately held back manufacturing activities in their countries and that vigorous action is needed to correct this imbalance.

Most developing countries have relied upon the private sector to carry the burden of increasing manufacturing activity. Governments have conceived their main role to be that of introducing policy measures that will encourage the private sector to undertake new and expanded industrial production. The main technique used for this purpose is the policy of import substitution. Protective tariffs and quantitative restrictions are imposed on imports of manufactures in order to raise the domestic price of these goods and make local production profitable. Since the development of domestic manufacturing industries usually requires heavy imports of capital goods and materials, governments also often encourage these industries by making the needed foreign exchange available at favorable terms. Still other governmental means of stimulating industry are: the creation of industrial development banks that make low interest, long-term loans; the provision of cheap electric power and other essential services; and the establishment of extensive labor-training facilities. But the key policy used to stimulate domestic industry has been to keep foreign products out of domestic markets.

In some instances it is quite apparent that the justification for a particular industrial activity is political and not economic. The economist should make clear just what the economic costs of the project are, but once this has been done and it is still decided to undertake the activity, there is not much more that can be said. Many of the import-substitution activities that are being undertaken so vigorously are, however, justified on economic grounds. The major argument used for this purpose is the traditional infant-industry case set forth by the classical economists. J. S. Mill long ago made the definitive presentation.[1]

The superiority of one country over another in a branch of production often arises only from having begun it sooner. There may be no inherent advantage on one part, or disadvantage on the other, but only a present superiority of acquired skill and experience. A country which has this skill and experience yet to acquire, may in other respects be better adapted to the production than those which were earlier in the field. . . . But it cannot be expected that individuals should, at their own risk, or rather to their certain loss, introduce new manufacture, and bear the burden of carrying it on until the producers have been educated up to the level of those with whom the processes are traditional. A protecting duty, continuing for a reasonable time, might sometime be the least inconvenient mode in which the nation can tax itself for the support of such an experiment.

It is useful to distinguish two types of labor training that a firm may undertake. The first concerns training labor in ways that

---

[1] J. S. Mill, *Principles of Political Economy*, Boston: Little and Brown, 1848, Vol. II, Bk. X, p. 495.

are useful only to the particular firm, such as teaching workers how to run a particular type of inventory-control system. The firm can recover the costs of training this type of labor by paying the workers, after their training period, somewhat less than their increased marginal productivity. There is no danger of losing them to other firms as long as they are receiving more than their initial wage: the figure that represents what they can earn elsewhere. The firm may not earn a profit during the training period, but if the activity is worthwhile for the economy as a whole, it will more than make this up afterwards. There is no reason to protect such a firm during its early stage of productive activity as long as capital markets are available in which to borrow at competitive rates. A tariff would merely attract too many firms to be efficient from a social viewpoint. In the absence of perfect capital markets, however, a protective tariff can increase profits for firms entering the field and thus provide them with more funds for training. But the unfavorable effects of this on saving and investment in other parts of the economy and the use of more efficient alternative methods of obtaining the capital funds must be carefully considered.

A second type of labor training is of a generalized nature, such as training an electrician who would be useful to many industries. In this case it will not be sensible for any firm to incur the costs of training this labor. As Mill noted, it will involve certain losses, since as soon as the worker is trained he must be paid his full marginal product or else another firm will hire him away. But if this is true the firm will never be able to recover its training costs. A tariff will not help this condition, however. It raises the internal price of the product and makes production in the industry more profitable, but any firm that pays the cost of training labor will lose this labor in competing with other firms for these profits. Nevertheless, there still will be a market force that tends to bring about the training of the workers. It will be in the interest of the workers themselves to pay for their own training by accepting wages during their training period that are less than their contribution to production. Doctors during their internship illustrate this type of response. Alternatively, workers will attend schools where they pay to obtain their training, on the theory that additional earnings during their working lifetime will compensate them. Of course, this conclusion is based on the assumptions of adequate foresight on the part of the workers and of perfect capital markets from which they can borrow funds at the competitive rate. Since neither of these is likely to hold completely in a developing country, there is a good case for government subsidization of the training of workers for generalized skills. In this labor-training case, as well as the first one considered, it is the probable existence of imperfect markets that warrants deliberate government attempts to encourage manufacturing activity.

Another argument for actively encouraging manufacturing which is also based on market imperfections, is the existence of surplus labor in agriculture. More particularly, suppose that those working on family farms are receiving incomes equal to their average productivity rather than a lower figure equal to their marginal productivity. Since wages in manufacturing will have to be at least as high as agricultural earnings in order to attract workers, it follows that there will be too few employed in manufacturing in terms of achieving the highest national product possible. The institutional arrangement whereby family farm workers receive their average rather than their marginal product prevents the market mechanism from operating efficiently. Protective tariffs, or, what is even more efficient, a labor subsidy to manufacturing firms, can be justified on economic grounds. As a matter of fact, even if the difference between the marginal productivity of labor in agriculture and industry is caused by the wage-raising actions of industrial unions, an expansion of industrial output is called for on economic grounds. But the best way of handling this type of inefficiency is to try to eliminate it directly rather than partly to offset it by countervailing measures.

There is no doubt that in its early stages the policy of import substitution was highly successful in bringing about a rapid rise in manufacturing activity. But it has not proved to be the catalyst for sound and continuing industrialization that many planners had initially hoped. Instead, many developing nations have become enmeshed in a web of industrial inefficiency from which they find it very difficult to free themselves.

The typical sequence of economic events associated with the policy of all-out import substitution has been as follows. Local entrepreneurs and foreign direct investors readily establish final-stage processing plants in various manufacturing lines when these activities are made profitable by high levels of protection from imports. However, because of the small size of local markets and high cost of labor in efficiency terms, the value added in production by domestic firms must be protected at rates of 50%, 100%, and often much more so that such activities can be made profitable. Consequently, there is a significant rise in the costs of import-competing goods. A heavy demand is also placed upon the supply of foreign exchange earned by existing export industries in the form of purchases of capital equipment needed for the new plants as well as raw materials and semimanufactured components required for current production.

As more and more new industries are established, the early import-substituting industries that use the outputs of the new industries as inputs into production find their costs rising and turn to the government for further protection. Usually the government responds by raising import barriers still higher. However, in so doing it begins to build a patchwork of elaborate and often inconsistent import restrictions that are costly to administer and increasingly hamper the entire domestic sector. One group that is particularly harmed by the controls is exporters. Traditional exporters find it increasingly difficult to obtain the foreign exchange needed to purchase their key equipment requirements. Moreover, they are faced with rising costs as import-competing industries bid up wages and they are required to purchase some of their inputs from high-cost domestic producers. Since prices in international markets do not also rise, the developing country is soon faced with a decline in the value of its exports.

As the control system becomes more and more cumbersome and burdensome for all sectors, pressure arises for its rationalization. One suggestion usually made is to devalue the country's currency and at the same time remove some of the export subsidies and quantitative import restrictions. Increasing the price of foreign currencies in terms of the local currency is equivalent to introducing a certain percentage duty on all imports *and* a subsidy of the same percentage on exports. Unfortunately, at this stage it becomes apparent that the degree of import protection varies greatly from industry to industry. An across-the-board devaluation coupled with the elimination of all controls will make it impossible for some industries that are very highly protected to compete successfully with imports. Since these industries are often important employers of the already surplus, urban labor force, governments find it very difficult to take the action needed to eliminate these high-cost industries. Yet, further import substitution (and especially a gradual shift towards exporting manufactures) tends to be stymied by the continued existence of these industries. Potential export industries that use the outputs of the protected industries as intermediate inputs are, in a sense, forced to pay an export tax on their production. The inefficient import-competing industries also tie up the economy's scarce supplies of foreign exchange, skilled labor, and entrepreneurial talent.

Another policy that is often followed in order to offset some of the inefficiencies associated with large-scale import substitution is to subsidize exports of manufactured goods. It is hoped that access to international markets will enable many domestic manufacturing industries to take advantage of the economics of large-scale production and thus in time become sufficiently efficient to no longer require subsidies.

Besides subsidizing exports of manufactured goods themselves, the developing countries have urged the developed nations to grant tariff preferences on the exports of these goods from developing economies. In other words, the developed countries would levy higher import duties on manufactures against other developed countries than against those from developing countries. The justification given for this policy is the infant-industry argument. In this case, however, the way to overcome the drawbacks of inexperience and lack of training is preferential tariff treatment in world-export markets.

Since this policy involves abandoning the principle of treating all nations equally in commercial matters, a principle that has been the cornerstone of postwar commercial relations, there has been a vigorous debate over the preference proposal. The developing countries claim that the infant-industry argument is applicable and is as valid in an international context as a domestic one. Moreover, they say that the developed countries will hardly notice an increase in exports of manufactures from the developing countries, since these exports are such a small fraction of their market. Indeed, to allay any fears of market disruption, the advocates of preference are willing to establish tariff quotas on individual items. If imports from developing nations exceed these quota levels, they will be subject to the regular duty.

Opponents of the scheme point out that the benefits are likely, in the foreseeable future, to accrue mainly to a few developing countries who already are exporting manufactures and do not need infant-industry help. In addition, the major part of the burden of subsidizing the developing nations is likely to fall upon a few developed countries. Counties with high duties will be the most attractive markets under a simple preferential scheme, and countries that are important exporters of simple manufactures will suffer the greatest loss in their share of developed country markets. A preferential scheme can, according to its opponents, easily lead to elaborate quantitative regulations that may spread to all aspects of international trade and reverse the postwar trend toward freer world trade. One aspect of this possible reversal of the free-trade movement is that it will be in the interests of developing countries to oppose general tariff reductions, since this will erode their margin of preference. Still another objection to the preference proposal concerns the possibility of adverse political consequences. An openly discriminatory scheme such as tariff preferences is almost bound to generate ill feelings on the part of some countries. These can seriously affect international relations in political as well as economic matters.

One argument against granting tariff preference, which appears to be sound but in fact is not, is that the tariffs levied by advanced countries are already low on many of the simply processed manufactures on which developing countries tend to specialize, and therefore these tariffs are not important trade barriers. This argument neglects the point that the degree of protection afforded to an industry depends not only upon the duty on the industry's output but also upon both the relative importance of material inputs in the value of the industry's output and the duties on these inputs. Suppose, for example, two commodities being produced in a developed country sell for $1 each under free-trade conditions. Assume that production in the first industry involves a relatively small amount of additional processing of materials and that the cost of the industry's product can be broken down into $.80 worth of internationally traded material inputs and $.20 worth of value that is added by the labor and capital directly employed in the industry. On the other hand, in the second industry say the cost of internationally traded material inputs amounts to only $.40 and the value added by primary factors to $.60. Under the assumption of completely elastic import supply curves, a 10% duty on both products will raise their prices to $1.10. If no duties are imposed on intermediate inputs, value added per unit of output rises to $.30 (i.e., $1.10 − $.80) in the first industry and $.70 (i.e., $1.10 − $.40) in the second industry. Since value added is initially $.20 and $.60, respectively, in the two industries, the percentage increase in value added in the first industry is 50% [i.e. ($.30 − $.20)/ $.20 × 100], and only 17% [i.e. (.70 − $.60)/$.60 × 100] in the second. This means that for a given rate of duty the degree of protection given to primary factors in the industry involving less processing activity is much larger than in the industry in which the processing activity is more elaborate. Therefore, low duties in the first type of industry may entail as much or more protection to primary factors as high duties in complex productive activities.

The United States opposed the preference proposal when it was first made at the United Nations Conference on Trade and Development (UNCTAD) in 1964. However, this position was gradually modified and by the time of UNCTAD–II held in 1968, the United States supported a resolution calling for the early establishment of a preference scheme. Progress towards an agreement acceptable to both the developed and developing nations has been exceedingly slow thus far, however. The recent action by the European Community of unilaterally granting preferences to the developing countries is likely to hasten the granting of preferences by other developed countries.

It is difficult to make a sound overall assessment of the import-substitution policies followed by most countries during the last several years. In view of the relatively slow growth in world demands for the traditional, primary-product exports of the developing nations and the need to find employment for a rapidly growing labor force in these countries, the strategy of attempting to shift the structure of production towards manufacturing activities has clearly been the appropriate one for the developing nations as a group. However, there does seem to be growing evidence that some countries have pushed the policy of import substitution too far in terms of their long-run employment and income goals. Industrial growth in these countries has slowed down because of the widespread production inefficiencies engendered by an overly ambitious import-substitution policy. On the other hand, in such countries as Korea, Taiwan, Mexico, and Malaya that have not provided very high levels of protection to manufacturing industries, growth rates of the outputs of manufactures, exports of manufactured goods, and total per capita income have continued at relatively high levels. However, there are so many other variables affecting development performance that one cannot be sure whether different import-substitution policies are significant in accounting for these differences. But more and more studies seem to be supporting this view.

III. INFRASTRUCTURE

Economists have long advised governments to intervene in the market mechanism in such areas as transportation, communications, public health, and education. These and similar fields are the ones in which capital indivisibilities, collective goods, technological externalities, and imperfect markets are most likely to exist and cause divergences between private and social profitability. Moreover, the services produced in these sectors enter as significant inputs for a wide range of goods and services produced in the economy. Consequently, should production be at socially inefficient levels in these key industries, development can be substantially held back over the entire economy.

No useful generalization can be made about whether a developing country should concentrate on building roads or irrigation projects or electric-power plants. It all depends on the particular circumstances in the country at the time. We must do the kind of project evaluation outlined in the preceding chapter to determine the answer. There is, however, one category of expenditures on social overhead capital that has been much discussed recently and on which some comment will be made. It is the field of education. Some of the recent analytical work done on the subject within the last few years has already been summarized in Chapter 5.

The interesting point about education is that it has replaced capital accumulation in the thinking of some economists as *the* key factor in economic development. Development planners increasingly regard a lack of skills and knowledge as more of a growth barrier than a lack of savings. It is a welcome change that they are taking a much less mechanical view of the development process than is to be obtained from simple models of capital accumulation. They are coming to appreciate the importance of the qualitative aspects of the population, especially its skill and entrepreneurial abilities.

One result of this new emphasis has been to increase substantially the public outlay on education—an outlay that as a proportion of national income is now comparable to that prevailing in developed countries. The enthusiasm for education in the developing countries is not simply a matter of economics. Better education is a symbol of freedom and a release from the constraints of ignorance and backwardness that have held back these people for many years.

In general, this great emphasis on education is to be applauded on economic, sociological, and political grounds. There is, however, a danger that these countries may be relying too much on it. For a while, all we thought we had to do to get an economy to "take-off" into a period of "sustained growth" was to raise its saving ratio above 10%. Many developed countries have achieved this saving level and still are plagued by all sorts of development problems. Now some countries are acting as if education will solve all their problems. But it is worth repeating that there seems to be no simple, primrose path to development.

In determining educational policy, careful attention must, as Hla Myint has stressed,[2] be given to the demand as well as to the supply side. For example, a standard lament about certain developing economies is that they have too many lawyers working only a few hours a day. What these countries need, it is said, is more engineers and technicians who will really be useful. Yet,

---

[2] Hla Myint, *The Economics of the Developing Countries*, New York: Frederick A. Praeger, 1965, pp. 173–177.

one reason young people become lawyers rather than engineers is because they can earn more as lawyers. Any politician who thinks that the best way to change this situation is by nationalistic appeals is in for a rude shock. The price system should be used to increase the number of engineers, if that is what is needed. But just turning out a lot of engineers is not going to accomplish much unless it is accompanied by other measures that ensure that these individuals will be absorbed into particular industries. For example, other supply bottlenecks must be overcome. But it is most important to make sure that there is a demand for the products of these particular industries, since, as no development planner should ever forget, the demand for any productive factor stems from the demand for the outputs it produces.

Probably the most difficult decision that must be made in the education field is the extent to which available resources should be devoted to mass education and the extent to which they should be used for selective, specialized training. There are usually strong political pressures for at least a minimum of education for all. Beyond a minimum, it is possible for political and educational leaders to shape the pattern of expenditures on schooling. If they try to follow the mass-education approach in these levels, they run the risk of using their scarce supply of teachers to turn out poorly trained, unimaginative students. To provide dynamic competent public officials and business leaders, it might be better to concentrate on smaller numbers of students. So far, neither educators nor economists have come to any firm judgments about this matter.

IV. POPULATION POLICY

As noted in Chapter 1, one of the most striking characteristics of most developing nations is their very rapid rates of population growth. In contrast to a growth rate of about 1.0% in the developed countries, population in the developing nations is increasing at 2.5% annually. Since a prime objective of these latter countries is to raise per capita income, promoting this goal by officially encouraging smaller families is an obvious policy option.

There seems to be little doubt that a decline in fertility rates will raise per capita income. The initial impact of such a decline is to reduce the already high ratio of dependents to those in the labor force. This not only raises per capita income directly but also is likely to create favorable secondary effects on living standards by increasing labor efficiency through higher nutritional levels and by raising labor productivity through higher saving and investment levels. The eventual slackening in the growth rate of the labor force is also likely to have a favorable effect on per capita income in most developing nations since rural underemployment and urban unemployment is already a serious problem in these countries. Furthermore, the general quality of life will tend to improve (or, at least, will stop deteriorating) with a reduction in population growth.

Within the last decade there has been a marked increase in efforts to spread family planning in the less developed countries. In India, for example, the national family planning program was greatly expanded in 1965 and a goal was established of reducing the birth rate from 40 to 25 per 1,000 population "as expeditiously as possible." Pakistan has also embarked upon a massive program designed to reduce the family size. Ambitious family planning efforts in Singapore, Hong Kong, Taiwan, and Korea have already contributed to a significant decline in fertility rates, and even outside of Asia in such countries as the United Arab Republic, Columbia, and Mexico modest efforts to reduce the birth rate through planning are under way.

It has proved to be a difficult task, however, to institute significant population-control programs and make them successful. In some parts of the developing world, particularly Latin America, family planning has been vigorously opposed on religious grounds. But there are also a number of other major obstacles to reducing birth rates. Some political leaders in comparatively small countries believe that their international political strength and military power will be seriously diminished if their population growth slackens. Ethnic tensions within a country also sometimes make it difficult to inaugurate successful family planning programs. Each group is concerned lest family planning be adopted only by their own group, thereby reducing its political influence. Rapid population growth is also a "low visibility" problem. Infants remain at home and do not consume much food. They only become visible when and if they enter school or, much later, when they enter the labor force. Even then the consequences are not usually dramatically obvious. Moreover, compared to such programs as building better roads, housing, irrigation facilities, hospitals, etc. family planning activities produce much less immediate results.

Considerable difficulties have also been encountered in convincing husbands and wives to limit their family size even when contraceptive devices are readily available. In a poor rural country with high death rates, it is economically rational to have a large number of children in order to ensure a sufficient number of workers for the family farm as well as enough adults to take care of the parents when they are ill or old. Rapidly declining death rates and urbanization weaken the need for a high birth rate for these reasons, but there is usually a significant time lag before this fact is realized by most of the population. Moreover, even when there is a general desire on the part of couples to limit the size of their families, it has often proved difficult to obtain compliance with birth control instructions on a steady basis. Large-scale public campaigns designed to change people's motivations seem a necessary part of any successful family planning program. Furthermore, the simpler the technique for controlling births the more likely it is that the program will succeed. In this connection, the recent emphasis on birth control pills and the intrauterine contraceptive device greatly improves the prospects for reducing fertility rates in the developing countries. Since most experts believe that the Green Revolution buys the developing countries an additional 15 to 30 years before outright famines occur, it is clear that efforts to institute effective programs of population control must rank at the top of the list of policy priorities in most developing countries.

8

Financing Development

It may be true in developed countries that "there is nothing more certain than death and taxes," but in developing nations perhaps "inflation" should replace "taxes" in the proverb. The record of increases in consumer prices in some of the most inflationary of the developing countries between 1963 and 1970 is as follows: Uruguay 1,940%, Brazil 638%, Argentina 284%, Chile 454%, and Korea 143%. By contrast, the degree of inflation in most major developed countries was about 30% in the same period.

I. THE INFLATION PROBLEM

The inflation story usually goes something like this. After a government has obtained all the revenue that it can obtain from taxation and foreign sources, it still has insufficient funds to carry out the development program that it is committed to undertake. As a result, it borrows money from the banking system, which simply creates it. In much the same manner described by Schumpeter, the government then "raids the circular flow" with the newly created money and purchases the particular types of labor services, raw materials, and capital goods that it needs. Because of the rigidities and supply inelasticities so characteristic of developing countries, the prices of these productive factors rise significantly as the government attempts to bid them away from their existing uses. Putting the matter another way, these inelasticities mean that the government must borrow extensively to secure all the resources it needs.

At the outset of the inflation process, the forced-saving mechanism usually works reasonably well. The government bids resources away from consumption-goods industries and increases the volume of investment. However, unless idle resources are pulled into the production stream via the inflationary process, this increase in investment can be accomplished only by reducing the standard of living of some people. There may be a certain amount of slack that can be taken up in this way, but under-employment in most developing countries cannot be eliminated merely by expanding aggregate demand. Consequently, the burden of inflation falls upon those groups whose money incomes lag behind the rise in prices. These usually include government employees, many classes of industrial workers, and fixed income recipients.

If the increased consumption output resulting from the investment activity came on the market before those suffering a real income decline could do very much in the way of resisting their loss, the inflationary process conceivably could end at this point. It would simply mean that these groups had temporarily reduced their consumption standards to permit additional capital accumulation. This outcome is not typical, however. First of all, governments are not interested in raising investment levels just for a short period. To carry out their programs they must increase investment activity over several years. The gestation period of many of such activities as power projects and education facilities is also quite lengthy. Furthermore, not many income groups will wait very long before exercising their economic and political powers in an effort to restore their purchasing power. Industry and government are soon faced with the prospect of strikes and sometimes even riots unless they raise the money earnings of these groups. They, consequently, turn to still more bank borrowing to meet these demands. Since this increase in the money supply acts to increase prices still more, government and industry must continue to step up their borrowings to carry out their own investment programs. In short, another inflationary spiral it set off.

Unless the banks are willing and able to create additional

credit, the entire process gets stopped in its tracks. At this point, the political pressures for continued expansion are so strong that the government takes actions permitting banks to continue to lend. The reserve ratio of the banks may be lowered or the banks may be able to count as part of their reserves the bonds sold to them by the government when it wants additional funds.

One of the most striking effects of inflation is a shift in production patterns within the economy. Consider the international sector, for example. As internal prices rise, domestic purchasers increasingly turn to foreign sources for the goods that they desire. Not only do imports rise, but export proceeds usually fall. Local labor and material costs go up, whereas world export prices remain about the same, unless the country in question is a large supplier in the world market. If it is not, more and more domestic producers are squeezed out of export production, and exchange earnings decline.

All of this could be avoided if the country depreciates its currency internationally at the same pace as this currency depreciates domestically. The cost of imports then would increase as fast as domestic prices, and exporters would receive enough domestic currency in return for the foreign exchange that they earn to cover their higher domestic costs. Most governments are reluctant, however, to devalue their currency under inflationary conditions. For one thing, they are afraid that this will lead to even more inflationary pressure. But they also find it convenient to rely on quantitative controls over foreign exchange to ensure that expanding industries obtain needed imports of raw materials and capital goods. In a free market for foreign exchange these industries may not be able to outbid those who want imported consumer goods.

As consumer-goods imports are curtailed by quantitative controls, spending pressures are deflected into the domestic markets for these goods. The rise in these prices attracts investors who, in turn, try to bid resources away from other industries. The longer prices continue to rise, the more important it becomes for investors to consider whether prices in a particular line will rise as fast or faster than the general price level. Such price behavior, unfortunately, is not likely to be correlated with productivity prospects in these industries under stable price conditions. One way to hedge against inflation is, of course, to send funds out of the country. If this is blocked, real estate investment or the stock-piling of standardized commodities are good alternatives. The hoarding of gold and other precious metals is another way frequently used to try to maintain the real value of one's assets. Many of the social overhead investments that the government initially undertook to stimulate development become the least desirable investments from a private point of view. If there had been some privately financed investment activity in these areas, it is likely to be cut back, and this puts an even heavier burden on the government program.

Nobody denies these adverse effects of inflation. But there are still at least three main questions to be answered. Is inflation inevitable in developing countries? Granting all of the distorting effects of inflation, is it not true that a country is still likely to end up with a higher investment and growth rate? How can inflation be stopped?

Writers stressing the inevitability of inflation (or, as they really mean, the necessity of inflation) emphasize the resource immobilities mentioned earlier. They argue that unemployment would occur in some sectors of the economy if the extra funds needed to bring about the resource shifts associated with development did not represent newly created credit but instead were obtained by reducing spending for other resources. Some writers also use the argument that, since voluntary domestic savings plus foreign aid will be insufficient to enable the developing nations to break out of their low-level, equilibrium trap, it is necessary to take the risks associated with the forced-savings method of development financing. Both of these contentions, however, do not seem to be supported by recent development history. Mexico and Venezuela are among a number of developing countries which have achieved an impressive growth record in recent years without considerable inflation. Not many economists become concerned over a price rise of 2% per year; the real issue is whether the kind of price increases that have occurred in Chile, Argentina, and Brazil are necessary. On this point, the evidence is clearly against the inflationists.

Whether inflationary financing actually works for more than a short period is more difficult to answer. The case of Brazil is often cited in support of the argument that it does. Although the data are not as complete as we would desire, it does appear that the forced-savings method of financing development has played an important role in Brazil's rapid growth in the postwar period. The real earnings of industrial and rural workers have lagged behind the growth of industrial and agricultural output, and the distribution of income has thus shifted in favor of profit receivers. Since the propensity to save by this income group is greater than that of wage earners, net savings in the economy have risen. The workers did not have the economic or political power to offset this unfavorable income redistribution. The Brazilian experience also does not indicate any drastic misallocation of resources.

In contrast to Brazil, the inflation experience in Argentina and Chile seems to support the position that forced saving is not a net contributor to growth for long. In these countries, workers are better organized economically and politically and have been better able to prevent a long-run redistribution of income against themselves. Consequently, the misallocation impact of large price increases and their adverse effects on incentives seems to have more than offset the redistributive forces associated with inflation in the postwar period.

Even if two economic and financial experts agree on the harmful effects of inflation, they might still disagree on how to stop it. One may argue that inflation can be easily stopped by appropriate monetary and fiscal restraints without causing serious adjustment problems or slowing down the rate of development. On the contrary, this expert might argue that the growth rate would increase. The other expert might claim that such a policy would, in fact, sharply curtail existing rates of development because of the high degree of resource inflexibility in developing countries. But more than this, he is likely to maintain that it is naive from a political viewpoint to think that a few monetary authorities can carry out a deflationary action. Inflation is a manifestation of social as well as economic maladjustments. The basic inflation problem can only really be solved through economic development, which increases resource flexibility, and by means of fundamental social reforms aimed at reducing tensions and antagonisms among income groups.

Like most matters of this sort, the truth seems to lie somewhere in between these two positions. There have been many unsuccessful attempts to halt inflation in Latin America. They failed, not because somebody lacked the technical knowledge concerning how to stop inflation, but because political pressures prevented this knowledge from being fully utilized. This is not to say that nothing can ever be done. At a minimum, it is reasonable to expect those countries where inflation has clearly hurt development to plan for and carry out long-run stabilization programs. The full power and prestige of international organizations on which the developing countries are represented should be used to help accomplish this goal.

In applying monetary constraints to inflation, the developing countries cannot simply use the same techniques that have proved successful in developed countries. Open-market operations and changing the rediscount rate, for example, are not very effective control devices in developing countries. The market for government securities is too narrow for open market operations to be effective, and the banks' frequent practice of keeping excess reserves makes changes in the rediscount rate ineffective as a control measure during the early stages of inflation. The wide fluctuation in export earnings and, therefore, bank reserves is another factor that makes credit control difficult.

Several monetary techniques are used to get around these drawbacks. They are all designed to control the availability of credit directly. One technique is to require all commercial banks to hold some proportion of their reserves in special government securities. This makes reserve ratio changes more effective and provides the foundation for open-market operations. Selective controls over particular sectors are also employed effectively in many developing countries. These include restrictions on consumer credit, limitations on the volume of real estate loans, and quantitative measures restricting loans for nonessential imports.

II. TAXATION

Since deficit financing is a highly uncertain and often dangerous way to obtain revenue and since foreign aid is usually limited, governments have to face up to the harsh reality that most development revenues must come from standard domestic sources.

Borrowing from the public and reinvesting the profits of public enterprises are useful ways of obtaining funds, but the main method generally is taxation.

As in the monetary field, developing countries cannot merely follow the tax policies of developed countries. Take, for example, the income tax. In many developed countries it is the central government's major source of tax revenue. In developing countries, indirect taxes such as excise and sales taxes usually are much more important. There are good reasons for this difference. There is frequently a large, nonmonetary sector in developing economies where it is impossible to accurately assess the income levels of individual producers. Even small businessmen and professionals in the monetary sector often do not keep the kind of records needed to establish an adequate income tax system. Furthermore, in many countries the tradition of complying with the tax laws by reporting income accurately simply does not exist. Nor can one rely too much on the efficiency and honesty of those appointed to administer the tax laws. Nevertheless, it seems clear that as urbanization and industrialization proceed, developing countries must shift more towards direct taxes if they are to meet their revenue requirements. The income tax is already a very useful tool for obtaining revenue from large foreign and domestic corporations and from those earning money wages, but it must be extensively supplemented by other tax devices if all groups in the economy are to be reached. Even as a means of raising revenue from business, it has the serious drawback of discouraging private investment, both domestic and foreign.

One suggestion for overcoming the difficulties of assessing and reporting income in sectors where economic activity is carried on by barter is to list all of the income-producing assets of each family and then to levy taxes on this basis. Local authorities would first determine, for example, how many coffee trees, cows, and acres of corn each family owns. Then, on the basis of records from agricultural experts, they would assign a certain earnings capacity to each type of asset within a given region. This would enable them to fix an income level for each family and then levy a tax on it.

An obvious supplement to the income tax that also has important social and economic benefits is the real estate tax. In countries where large amounts of land are owned by a few, a property tax is a simple device for tapping the income of this wealthy group. If rates are set high enough, the tax will also force large landowners to sell off parts of their holdings. Furthermore, these high rates will tend to discourage the undesirable shift to real estate investments characteristic of inflationary periods. Unfortunately, in many of the Latin American countries where these points are relevant, real estate taxes are low. Large landowners are one of the most politically powerful groups in these countries, and they have successfully resisted attempts to raise property taxes. In many other countries, however, real estate taxes are a major source of government revenue. They are always difficult to administer, but they can be an important method of using the economic surplus in agriculture for development purposes.

Another method used to raise revenue in the agricultural sector, as well as in other primary-product industries, is export taxation. The drawback of this tax, however, is that it reduces foreign exchange earnings if the demand for the country's exports is elastic. Of course, if a country's share of world exports of a particular primary product should be large, the outcome is likely to be quite different. The reduction in domestic supply caused by this tax is likely to result in a more than proportionate increase in the product's world price, and the country's export earnings then will actually increase. The export tax in this circumstance is a convenient device for exploiting a country's monopoly power. Some commodity schemes that started out as marketing arrangements designed to stabilize prices paid to domestic producers have also turned into devices for restricting output and, in effect, taxing these producers. This has been accomplished by paying producers less than the world price over a period of time that covers several cyclical price fluctuations. Some countries using this technique have discovered, however, that their long-run curve has become more and more elastic as new supply sources have arisen under the stimulus of a high world price.

The basic source of tax revenue in most developing countries is consumption taxation. These taxes usually are regarded in developed countries as highly undesirable because of their regressive nature. But the previously mentioned difficulties with income, property, and export taxes leave no other important alternative tax source in developing countries. However, the regressivity of excise and sales taxes levied on consumption goods can be reduced somewhat by covering luxury items extensively. Nonetheless, developing countries usually are forced to sacrifice the equity principle of taxation in favor of revenue considerations.

III. FOREIGN ASSISTANCE: PRIVATE AND PUBLIC

Although it is hard to pinpoint the particular sources of economic development, there is considerable evidence to indicate that the receipt of external resources has been a major factor in accounting for recent rapid growth in such countries as Taiwan, Turkey, Korea, and Pakistan. Moreover, in countries that received less foreign assistance or where initial conditions were not so favorable for development (e.g., India), it has been shown that external resources can be used effectively in carrying out particular programs that help set the stage for periods of more rapid growth. However, as a recent international report on development assistance (the Pearson Report) emphasized, support for foreign aid is now flagging. Aid commitments by the American government, for example, are lower now than in 1962. American private investment in the developing countries has increased rapidly, but the total flow of public and private resources to the developing nations as a percent of gross national product declined for the United States between 1960 and 1970. This percentage also fell for such other major aid givers as France and the United Kingdom as well as for all the developed countries as a whole.

The waning interest in public foreign-assistance programs is based on several reasons. First, many individuals who traditionally strongly supported foreign aid have come to believe that such domestic problems as poverty and pollution must now take priority over foreign-assistance programs. Moreover, they are prepared to accept absolute cuts in foreign assistance in order to promote the solution of poverty and environmental problems.

Another factor contributing to the decline in enthusiasm for foreign aid is the widespread belief that much of the aid has been wasted by the recipients. This position not only covers the view that aid has been diverted to uses other than the intended purposes but, more important, that it has been used inefficiently or for low-priority social and economic goals. Some go much further and maintain that all foreign-aid programs by the developed countries are actually an imperialistic means of exploiting the peoples of the developing nations. According to those holding this view, public foreign assistance is, in particular, often used to prop up undemocratic regimes in the developing countries.

Those favoring an increase in foreign aid now stress the humanitarian objective much more than they did in the past. It is morally right for those who have to share with those who have not. Moreover, since we live in a world community of highly interdependent nations, our concern for human welfare must not be directed just to those residing within our own particular national boundaries. Rather, the recently increased awareness by most people of the problems of poverty coupled with a greater willingness to help the poor should, according to foreign-aid proponents, serve as a reason for expanding public assistance abroad rather than contracting it.

During the 1950's and 1960's the main argument used to persuade taxpayers to transfer part of their incomes to developing countries was that it was in their best self-interest to do so. However, it has become increasingly clear that many of the particular arguments behind this view are of dubious validity. At one time, for example, much was made of the point that aid increases United States exports and helps to open up new supplies of inexpensive raw materials. However, in comparison with the economic returns from spending aid funds domestically, these alleged benefits seem slight. It is true that aid funds are used to purchase capital equipment produced in the United States. But this equipment may well be used to replace imports of some other item from the United States. Or the firms established with this equipment may supply products that compete with United States exports in third markets. Similarly, if there is one field where private investment is likely to flow readily, given half a chance, it is export-oriented, raw material industries in which prices are rising because of a growing scarcity of these materials. Another economic argument sometimes used is that foreign aid enables developed countries to dispose of their agricultural surpluses and thus maintain employment and income levels in the rural sector. As far as the economics of maintaining farm incomes is concerned, this goal can be achieved just as easily with domestic measures that have the additional real income advantage of keeping the consumption of these goods within the surplus country. More generally, of course, the policy tends to prevent the internal adjustments that the existence of surpluses indicates to be necessary. The economic arguments for foreign aid that are based on narrow self-interest are, in short, not very strong ones.

There are also several noneconomic arguments that do not stand up very well. One popular view is that there is a direct relationship between foreign aid and the friendship of the people in the recipient country. If people in rural areas see a farmer using a tractor and know it came from America, they will feel kindly toward the United States. Such a reaction is, of course, possible, but so too is a quite different one. The farmer may have been able to purchase the tractor only because he borrowed the money to do so. In the process of having to pay this money back he may well begin to think that its price was too high in the first place, and that the Americans are lined up with those who are trying to squeeze out more and more of his hard-earned income. Those who work for the farmer are likely to regard the tractor as a device for displacing them or at least for enabling the owner to reduce their wages. Other farmers who do not obtain tractors think favoritism is being shown and blame it on the Americans. And thus it could go with almost everyone who is involved with the tractor. People may turn from being indifferent to being resentful of the country extending aid.

It was often contended in the past that as income levels rise in developing countries through foreign aid, the people of these countries will turn away from communism and embrace the democratic and capitalistic tradition of the "free world" bloc. This argument assumes that poverty breeds communism and that affluence is associated with democracy. There is more wishful thinking than solid empirical evidence behind this hypothesis. Poverty may be one factor contributing to discontent but clearly, as the experience of Cuba and even China indicates, there are many other complex social and political elements that constitute a set of conditions favorable for a communist take-over. Even the argument that foreign aid directly promotes peace and stability seems dubious. On the contrary, significant economic progress in the developing world usually involves a break with traditional social relations and may induce highly destabilizing political change.

The self-interest argument may, however, have some validity in a very broad, long-run sense. It must be recognized that the fundamental social, political, and economic changes set in motion by significant income growth from an initially low level will continue in the developing countries whether or not they receive additional foreign aid. One important aspect of these changes is the greater awareness and often greater dissatisfaction on the part of the masses of poor people within the less developed countries with the gap between their living standard and that enjoyed by most people in the developed nations, as well as by the higher income groups within their own countries. The increased dissatisfaction with their economic and social status frequently leads to violent and costly internal conflicts within the developing nations. Such turmoil tends to affect the economic interests of the developing countries adversely by disrupting international trade and damaging foreign investments. In addition, prolonged internal strife increases the chances that other less developed neighboring countries will become involved and that the major industrial powers will become enmeshed in dangerous crises as they vie with each other in extending or protecting their spheres of political influence. If foreign assistance can reduce these economic costs and political dangers by shortening the evolution of the developing countries into stable states based on broad internal political support, then this assistance is likely to be in the enlightened self-interests of the developed nations. Since the development process can be accelerated by the inflow of resources from abroad and since the internal conflicts are partly related to development levels, there would thus seem to be a possible case for foreign aid on these grounds. However, whether in fact the actual foreign aid provided promotes the long-run interest of the developed nations depends on a number of specific matters relating to the nature of the aid. For example, the government of a developing country may use the assistance in ways that intensify and prolong the conflict rather than mitigate it. Furthermore, there may be levels of foreign aid that are either too low or too high in terms of furthering the desired objective. These and other considerations make it difficult to generalize about the political and social effects of foreign assistance. Each country must be considered as a unique case.

Traditionally, foreign development assistance mainly consisted of private investment. Although still significant—averaging $5.5 billion between 1967 and 1969—this type of aid now amounts to somewhat less than one-half of all financial aid to the developing countries. There are two forms of private investment: direct investment, where managerial control goes along with capital outflow, and portfolio investment, where the purchase of foreign securities does not give control of the enterprise. Direct investment is the most important of the two types, making up about two-thirds of all private investment in the developing nations.

A striking feature of the pattern of private investment in the developing countries is that about one-half is in export-oriented, extractive industries. Furthermore, three-fourths of this is in the petroleum industry. Often the objection is raised that this type of investment develops natural resources and not people. Not only is the immediate and indirect employment impact small absolutely but often a substantial number of those who are employed come from abroad. Moreover, instead of serving as a training school and a point from which useful technological knowledge spreads to other sectors, foreign investment in natural-resource industries serves merely to train labor to highly specialized tasks and to disperse highly detailed technical knowledge. The developing countries are afraid that they will end up with their natural resources depleted and no compensating benefits for the rest of the economy. Many people in these countries also still vividly recall their colonial history and are fearful that private foreign investment will result in new economic and political exploitation.

Because of such fears, developing countries often impose controls and regulations on foreign investment. India, for example, welcomes foreign investment in manufacturing but not in trade or distribution. Foreign firms must also make provision for the training of Indian personnel in high technical and administrative positions and admit Indian capital at all stages of the venture. Limitations are also imposed by many countries on the earnings that can be taken out of their countries. Of course, another device used to regulate, if not deter, direct foreign investment is to impose high tax rates on the earnings of foreign enterprises.

What can be done to increase the flow of private capital funds and yet minimize the real or imagined concerns of the developing countries regarding the adverse consequences of foreign investment? Even though some of the fears of these countries seem to be based on the past and not the present, there is no doubt that they are real in a political sense and cannot be quickly eliminated simply by making a few studies showing the advantages of private investment. For at least the immediate future, certain restrictions designed to allay the fears of neo-colonialism in the developing countries are bound to remain in force. One way to deal with the adverse effects of these restrictions is to try to devise countermeasures that will encourage private investment and yet be politically acceptable. Policies fitting this approach that the developing countries can themselves promote are: setting low tax rates on the profits of foreign enterprises provided that the profits are reinvested in the economy; establishing a framework for joint ventures in which foreign investors gradually turn over the managerial control and majority ownership to local interests, and local workers are quickly trained to replace foreign personnel; making sure that in the lines where investment is desired, such complementary public facilities as transportation and communications are efficient; training labor in the generalized skills needed in these industries; and furnishing accurate information on factor and product markets within the economy. An important step developed countries can take in encouraging private investment is to expand the kind of insurance program adopted by the American government under which American investors are protected against loss due to expropriation, currency inconvertibility, and war. The greater use of Treaties of Friendship, Commerce, and

Navigation, which lay down reciprocal rules of conduct for the operation of foreign enterprises, and the adherence by more nations to the international convention on the Settlement of Investment Disputes are other cooperative means for promoting private foreign investment.

The recent stagnation in official development assistance is indicated by the fact that these resources grew only from $5.2 billion in 1961 to $6.4 billion in 1968. Aid of this type is especially welcomed by the developing nations because it provides funds for financial social overhead capital—an area which private foreign investors tend to avoid. However, as in the case of private investment, the developing countries are very sensitive to the possible political influence that individual developed countries may exercise over them in granting aid and low-interest loans. For this reason, there is now general agreement in the developed and developing nations that more aid should be channeled through such multilateral agencies as the World Bank, the Inter-American Development, and the Asian Development Bank. Aid from multilateral organizations has recently grown rapidly in percentage terms, but bilateral assistance still accounts for almost 90% of official development assistance.

9

Concluding Remarks

I. THEORIES AND POLICIES

Like so many modern problems, the urgency of economic development as a social issue is out of proportion to our knowledge about development as an economic process. Nevertheless, although we are still a long way from a general theory of development, significant advances have been made in recent years towards a better understanding of key factors and relationships in economic growth. Much of the analytical progress can best be characterized as a rejection of simple and extreme views concerning the nature of development patterns and a growing awareness of their complexity. At the same time, there is now greater confidence that we know enough about these processes to be able to make substantial contributions towards alleviating poverty in this generation.

One relationship being repeatedly verified in developing countries is that the great majority of the people respond positively to economic incentives. When cash market opportunities improve, the typical small farmer tends to respond by increasing production. Similarly, the supply curve of labor in less developed countries seems generally to be positively sloped. Since economic development via reliance upon the price system is the most inexpensive way for governments to carry out their development commitments, the mass of evidence indicating that most people respond favorably to economic incentives is a very hopeful sign.

127

Those who believe that most individuals in developing countries possess limited wants and consequently work only to attain some "target" income either throw up their hands in despair about development prospects or argue that there is no hope until basic values and attitudes change. The latter course of action is at best very costly and time consuming and perhaps impossible to effectively carry out.

This does not mean that the cultural background of a country makes no difference. Quite clearly the environment in which individuals are raised plays an important role in the development process, especially in determining the supply of entrepreneurial ability. However, there seems to be a broad spectrum of cultures where economic development by means of free-market methods can flourish and from which at least a minimum amount of entrepreneurial talent can spring. No longer do most economists consider some particular culture as either essential for successful growth or a complete obstacle to such development.

At the same time, the accumulating evidence that most individuals respond favorably to economic incentive does not mean that merely providing economic opportunity is enough to achieve development. This is another simple view that is being discredited by recent experience. At one time many thought land reform to be the key to agricultural development. If a farmer owned his own land, it was thought that he would increase his market supplies of agricultural products. Now it is realized that land reform can be disastrous without concurrent programs to train farmers to direct their own agricultural operations, to provide credit facilities for new land owners, to furnish these farmers with appropriate market and technical information, etc. Likewise, changing a few prices set by marketing boards may be an important part of a rural development effort, but by no means should it be all there is to the program.

The rejection of some of the more extreme views about the nature of development carries over into the investment field. One widely held position has been that capital accumulation is the essence of development and that its pace can be increased more or less automatically by increasing the stock of material capital. A rather different, but similarly extreme notion is that, because of the complex interrelations among the detailed parts of the economy as well as the indivisibility of capital, a massive investment program covering all parts of the economy is needed for successful growth. Otherwise the economy will never break out of the vicious circle of poverty.

Recent growth experience indicates that development is not as simple as the first position suggests or as difficult as the second view implies. Simple models based upon aggregate capital-output ratios or even the investment and saving schedules of the neoclassical writers are not very useful for understanding the growth process in developing countries. A more microscopic analysis of these economies is needed. In particular, the leading industries in terms of their direct and indirect development impact must be analyzed as well as the interactions among major sectors of the economy. In other words, a disaggregative approach is essential for an adequate analysis of the growth process in less developed nations.

One merit of the big-push approach to investment planning is that it points to the significance of the demand and supply interactions among various industries and sectors. However, this analysis overemphasizes the importance of these repercussions. Its policy implications are that investment must be pushed forward in unison in almost all productive lines because of the crucial nature of these interactions. This does not seem to be necessary, judging by recent development history. A pattern of uneven growth in which one sector stimulates development in other sectors and itself is pulled forward by other sectors has proved to result in successful overall development efforts. Of course, no one sector can get too far ahead, but balance among sectors is a flexible relationship that must be maintained for successful development. The proponents of the big-push approach also overstressed the limitations that the indivisibility of capital impose on a more gradual and selective approach to investment efforts.

The notion that the accumulation of physical capital is the essence of economic development has come to be less widely held in recent years. Currently, investment in human capital in the form of expenditures on general education, vocational training, and health is being stressed on an especially important requirement. This emphasis is partly because more and more developing countries are gradually breaking through the traditional barrier of very low rates of capital accumulation. As they do this, they are finding that a lack of trained personnel is what slows down their growth rates. Undoubtedly, as educational levels improve, new constraints such as poor natural resources, will come to the forefront. We have learned enough now, however, to know that no one factor is the answer to more rapid growth. At certain times, one economic variable is more important than others but, over the long run, all factors of production combine to produce growth. Consequently, theories based mainly upon changes in one particular productive factor are strictly limited in their usefulness. The same is true of analyses suggesting that development always follows in some particular pattern or occurs in definite stages.

The trend towards rejecting simple, easy solutions to development problems is evident in the policy field. Such policy gimmicks as painless development via inflation or utilizing surplus labor in agriculture to achieve costless growth are no longer taken very seriously. They usually contain the kernel of a good policy notion, but they need to be considerably modified to become relevant for the real world. Highly detailed and elaborate planning also has not as yet proved itself to be very useful in government effort to accelerate growth. There may, some day, be a high payoff to these planning techniques but, as of now, development planning is still quite simple in the less developed, market economies.

Another encouraging trend in policy thinking within the developing countries is a growing awareness of the cost of development in economic and social terms. Too often in the past these countries viewed development as something that followed almost automatically from political independence and a moderate amount of foreign aid. They failed to appreciate that successful development at best is a relatively slow process and rests upon hard economic decisions at the domestic level. Moreover, even when successful, development brings a host of new problems. For example, the breaking-down of traditional attitudes and social organizations, which usually accompanies changes in productive structures, involves difficult personal readjustment problems. It is not enough for development leaders to think merely about steel mills and roads. They must also plan for new institutions and organizations to take over many of the social functions performed by the institutional arrangements that development destroys. Fortunately, in recent years the price tags attached to development, as well as its benefits, are being better appreciated.

We are at the point in development economics where there appears to be no single or simple policy prescriptions for successful growth. Some generalities can be made with respect to such general topics as commercial policy and fiscal policy and also about development policies in such broad economic sectors as agriculture and manufacturing, but each country must be considered in detail in order to formulate appropriate specific development policies. What is important, however, is that we are acquiring the kind of general knowledge needed to take the complex economic conditions of any particular country and formulate a set of analytically sound development policies for each country.

II. DEVELOPMENT PROSPECTS

The recent performance of the developing nations in aggregative terms has been encouraging. As indicated in Chapter 1, over the four-year period 1965–69, gross national product grew at a 5.8% annual rate in these countries. This is above the 5% target rate that the developing countries set for themselves by the end of this decade under a United Nations resolution, and is higher than the growth rate in developed countries. The ranking order according to per capita growth rate in the above period is reversed, however, due to a 2.6% annual growth rate of population in the developing countries compared to a 0.9% rate in the developed nations. This meant that per capita income rose 3.9% annually in developed countries and 3.2% in developing nations. The gap in per capita income has, in other words, continued to widen in recent years.

It is this widening gap that gives rise to concern about development prospects. Eliminating poverty in an absolute sense is a great and noble social goal, but it is not enough in these times. There is increasing political and social pressure to make narrowing the gap the goal of economic development. A world in which the rich get richer faster than the poor do is not likely to be politically stable and peaceful. However, reducing the income gap is going to be no easy task. Aggregate growth rates may be raised in the developing nations, but a more rapid expansion of the population in these countries is also a good possibility. In the meantime, as the developed countries gain greater experience in overcoming their unemployment problems, per capita growth rates may well exceed recent historical rates in these countries. Consequently it would seem that, if the per capita income gap is to be narrowed within the near future, it will require levels of both self-help and international cooperation going considerably beyond those of recent years.

Selected Bibliography

In addition to the books and articles mentioned in the text, the following list of books are useful for further study.

GENERAL SURVEYS

Bauer, P. T., and Yamey, B. S. *The Economics of Underdeveloped Countries*. Chicago: University of Chicago Press, 1957.

Bruton, H. J. *Principles of Development Economics*. Englewood Cliffs, N.J.: Prentice-Hall, 1965.

Enke, S. *Economics for Development*. Englewood Cliffs, N.J.: Prentice-Hall, 1963.

Hagen, E. *The Economics of Development*. Homewood, Ill.: Richard D. Irwin, 1968.

Higgins, B. *Economic Development*. Revised Edition. New York: W. W. Norton, 1968.

Kindleberger, C. P. *Economic Development*. Second Edition. New York: McGraw-Hill, 1965.

Lewis, W. A. *The Theory of Economic Growth*. Homewood, Illinois: Richard D. Irwin, 1955.

Maddison, A. *Economic Progress and Policy in Developing Countries*. New York: W. W. Norton, 1970.

Meier, G. M., and Baldwin, R. E. *Economic Development*. New York: John Wiley, 1957.

Myint, H. *The Economics of the Developing Countries*. New York: Frederick A. Praeger, 1965.

ANTHOLOGIES

Agarwala, A. N., and Singh, S. P. (eds.) *The Economics of Underdevelopment*. Fair Lawn, N.J.: Oxford University Press, 1958.

Eicher, C., and Witt, L. (eds.) *Agriculture in Economic Development*. New York: McGraw-Hill, 1964.

Meier, G. M. (ed.) *Leading Issues in Development Economics*. New York: Oxford University Press, 1970.

Morgan, T., and Betz, G. W. (eds.) *Readings in Theory and Practice*. Belmont, Calif.: Wadsworth, 1970.

Theberge, J. D. *Economics of Trade and Development*. New York: John Wiley, 1968.

SPECIAL TOPICS AND APPROACHES

Adelman, I., and Thorbecke, E. (eds.) *The Theory and Design of Economic Development*. Baltimore: The Johns Hopkins Press, 1966.

Anderson, C. A., and Bowman, M. J. (eds.) *Education and Economic Development*. London: Frank Cass and Co., Ltd., 1966.

Baran, P. *The Political Economy of Growth*. New York: Monthly Review Press, 1957.

Bowles, S. *Planning Educational Systems for Economic Growth*. Cambridge, Mass.: Harvard University Press, 1969.

Brown, L. R. *Seeds of Change: The Green Revolution and Development in the 1970's*. New York: Frederick A. Praeger, Inc., 1970.

Cairncross, A. K. *Factors in Economic Development*. London: George Allen and Unwin, 1962.

Clark, C. *Starvation or Plenty?* New York: Taplinger Publishing Co., 1970.

Coale, A. J., and Hoover, E. M. *Population Growth and Economic Development in Low-Income Countries*. Princeton: Princeton University Press, 1958.

de Vries, B. A. *Export Experiences of Developing Countries*. Baltimore: Johns Hopkins Press, for the 133 RD, 1967.

Diamond, W. *Development Banks*. Baltimore: Johns Hopkins Press, 1957.

Due, J. F. *Indirect Taxation in Developing Economics: The Role of Customs Duties, Excises, and Sales Taxes*. Baltimore: Johns Hopkins Press, 1970.

Ehrlich, P. R. *The Population Bomb*. New York: Ballantine Books, 1968.

Gerschenkron, A. *Economic Backwardness in Historical Perspective*. Cambridge, Mass.: Harvard University Press, 1962.

Gray, C. S. *Resource Flows to Less Developed Countries: Financial Terms and Their Constraints*. New York: Praeger Publishers, 1969.

Hagen, E. E. *Economic Planning*. Homewood, Illinois: Richard D. Irwin, 1963.

Hirschman, A. O. *Exit, Voice, and Loyalty—Responses to Decline in Firms, Organizations, and States*. Cambridge, Mass.: Harvard University Press, 1970.

Hirshman, A. O. *The Strategy of Economic Development*. New Haven, Conn.: Yale University Press, 1958.

Hoselitz, B. F. *Sociological Aspects of Economic Growth*. New York: The Free Press of Glencoe, 1960.

Johnson, H. G. *Economic Policies Toward Less Developed Countries.* Washington: The Brookings Institution, 1967.

Lary, H. B. *Imports of Manufactures from Less Developed Countries.* New York: Columbia University Press, 1968.

Leibenstein, H. *Economic Backwardness and Economic Growth.* New York: John Wiley, 1957.

Lewis, A. *Development Planning: The Essentials of Economic Policy.* New York: Harper and Row, 1966.

Little, I. M. D., and Clefford, J. M. *International Aid: A Discussion of the Flow of Public Resources from Rich to Poor Countries.* Chicago: Aldine Publishing Co., 1966.

Little, I. M. D., Scitovsky, T., and Scott, M. *Industry and Trade in Some Developing Countries: A Comparative Study.* London: Oxford University Press, 1970.

Magdoff, H. *The Age of Imperialism: The Economics of U.S. Foreign Policy.* New York: Modern Reader Paperbacks, 1969.

Maizels, A. *Exports and Economic Growth of Developing Countries.* Cambridge: The University Press, 1968.

Nurkse, R. *Problems of Capital Formation in Underdeveloped Countries.* New York: Oxford University Press, 1953.

Ohlin, G. *Population Control and Economic Development.* Paris: Development Centre of the OECD, 1967.

Papanek, G. F., ed. *Development Policy: Theory and Practice.* Cambridge, Mass.: Harvard University Press, 1968.

Pearson, L. B. *The Crisis of Development.* New York: Praeger Publishers, 1971.

Penrose, E. *The Large International Firm in Developing Countries: The International Petroleum Industry.* London: George Allen and Unwin, Ltd., 1968.

Prest, A. R. *Public Finance in Underdeveloped Countries.* New York: Frederick A. Praeger, 1963.

Schultz, T. W. *Economic Growth and Agriculture.* New York: McGraw-Hill, Inc., 1968.

Schultz, T. W. *Transforming Traditional Agriculture.* New Haven: Yale University Press, 1964.

Southworth, H. M., and Johnston, B. F. (eds.) *Agricultural Development and Economic Growth.* Ithaca, New York: Cornell University Press, 1967.

Thorbecke, E. (ed.) *The Role of Agriculture in Economic Development.* New York: National Bureau of Economic Research, 1970.

Tinbergen, J. *Development Planning.* New York: McGraw-Hill, 1967.

Warriner, D. *Land Reform and Development in the Middle East.* London: Oxford University Press, 1957.

Waterston, A. *Development Planning: Lessons of Experience.* Baltimore: The Johns Hopkins Press, 1965.

Wharton, C. R., Jr. (ed.) *Subsistence Agriculture and Economic Development.* Chicago: Aldine Publishing Co., 1970.

CASE STUDIES

Baer, W. *The Development of the Brazilian Steel Industry.* Nashville, Tenn.: Vanderbilt University Press, 1969.

Baer, W. *Industrialization and Economic Development in Brazil.* Homewood, Illinois: Richard D. Irwin, 1965.

Baldwin, G. B. *Planning and Development in Iran.* Baltimore: Johns Hopkins Press, 1967.

Baldwin, R. E. *Economic Development and Export Growth: A Study of Northern Rhodesia.* Berkeley and Los Angeles: University of California Press, 1966.

Barber, W. J. *The Economy of British Central Africa.* Stanford: Stanford University Press, 1961.

Bergsman, J. *Brazil: Industrialization and Trade Policies.* London: Oxford University Press, 1970.

Bhagwati, J. N., and Desai, P. *India: Planning for Industrialization.* London: Oxford University Press, 1970.

Diaz Alejandro, C. F. *Exchange-Rate Devaluation in a Semi-Industrialized Country: The Experience of Argentina, . . . 1955–1961.* Cambridge, Mass.: M.I.T. Press, 1965.

Edel, M. *Food Supply and Inflation in Latin America.* New York: Praeger Publishers, 1969.

Ellis, H. S. (ed.) *The Economy of Brazil.* Berkeley: University of California Press, 1969.

Golay, F. H. *The Philippines; Public Policy and National Economic Development.* Ithaca: Cornell University Press, 1961.

Halevi, N., and Klinov-Malul, R. *The Economic Development of Israel.* New York: Frederick A. Praeger, 1968.

Hsing, M., Power, J. H., and Sicat, G. P. *Taiwan and The Philippines: Industrialization and Trade Policies.* London: Oxford University Press, 1971.

Kamarck, A. M. *The Economics of African Development.* New York: Frederick A. Praeger, 1967.

Kilby, P. *Industrialization in an Open Economy: Nigeria, 1945–1966.* New York: Cambridge University Press, 1969.

Koo, A. Y. *The Role of Land Reform in Economic Development: A Case Study of Taiwan.* New York: Frederick A. Praeger, 1958.

Lewis, J. P. *Quiet Crisis in India.* Washington: Brookings Institution, 1962.

Lewis, S. R., Jr. *Economic Policy and Industrial Growth in Pakistan.* Cambridge, Mass.: M.I.T. Press, 1969.

Lewis, S. R., Jr. *Economic Policy and Economic Growth in Pakistan.* London: George Allen and Unwin, Ltd., 1969.

Lockwood, W. W. *The Economic Development of Japan.* Princeton: Princeton University Press, 1954.

Myrdal, G. *Asian Drama: An Inquiry into the Poverty of Nations.* New York: Pantheon Books, 1968.

Papanek, G. F. *Pakistan's Development: Social Goals and Private Incentives.* Cambridge, Mass.: Harvard University Press, 1967.

Perkins, D. H. *Market Control and Planning in Communist China.* Cambridge, Mass.: Harvard University Press, 1966.

Reynolds, C. W. *The Mexican Economy: Twentieth Century Structure and Growth.* New Haven and London: Yale University Press, 1970.

Reynolds, L. G., and Gregory, P., with Torruellas, L. M. *Wages, Productivity, and Industrialization in Puerto Rico.* Homewood, Illinois: Richard D. Irwin, 1965.

Roemer, M. *Fishing for Growth: Export-Led Growth in Peru, 1950–1967.* Cambridge, Mass.: Harvard University Press, 1970.

Rosen, G. *Democracy and Economic Change in India.* Berkeley and Los Angeles: University of California Press, 1966.

Snodgrass, D. R. *Ceylon: An Export Economy in Transition.* Homewood, Illinois: R. D. Irwin, 1966.

Stern, J. J., and Falcon, W. P. *Growth and Development in Pakistan, 1955–1969.* Cambridge, Mass.: Harvard University Center for International Affairs, 1970.

Stopler, W. *Planning Without Facts—Lessons in Resource Allocation from Nigeria's Development.* Cambridge, Mass.: Harvard University Press, 1966.

Strassman, W. B. *Technological Change and Economic Development: The Manufacturing Experience of Mexico and Puerto Rico.* Ithaca, New York: Cornell University Press, 1968.

Tanzer, M. *The Political Economy of International Oil and the Underdeveloped Countries.* Boston: Beacon Press, 1969.

Vernon, R. *The Dilemma of Mexico's Development.* Cambridge, Mass.: Harvard University Press, 1963.

Index